Once Upon An Island

Memories of a Swedish boy

By Axel Lindstrom

Sweden

Finland

Stockholm

Ormsö

Estonia

Once Upon An Island
First Printing
Copyright © 2003 by Axel Lindstrom

All rights reserved. Written permission must be secured from the author to use or reproduce any part of this book, except for brief quotations in critical reviews or articles.

ISBN 0-9740409-0-8
Library of Congress Control Number: 2003094561

Ravenwood Publishing
Gig Harbor, Washington

Printed in the United States

Dedicated to my wife, Karen
And
To my ancestors who left a legacy of solid family values

Acknowledgements

I wish to express my gratitude to the following people who helped me greatly:

To my sisters, Katharina Hedin and Elsa Seffers, for sharing memories and sending old letters, photos and documents, but more so, for their encouragement throughout the years

To Richard Rydén, Sven Rydén's grandson, for his diligent research, providing me with additional photos and information

To family and friends who offered their invaluable input

And last, but not least, my gratitude to my wife, Karen, for keeping the candle burning with typing, designing and editing; a quiet spark behind the scenes. But most of all, for believing in me.

Preface

My last day in the office went by quickly, with good-byes and thank-yous stretching into early evening. This chapter of my life, forty years of a rewarding medical practice, was now over.

A few weeks later, my sister Elsa called from Sweden. After talking about family news, Elsa excitedly told me of an old trunk she had found filled with pictures of our childhood. We began to reminisce about some of the hair-raising adventures we had lived through. Looking back, it seems impossible that we lived and grew up enjoying life without running water, electricity or telephone.

Inspired by her call, and since I now had the time, I decided to put a few stories down on paper. And, why not take a writing class, my wife suggested? I signed up, and at the end of the course, with encouragement from my instructor, I began to record some of my life experiences.

This book is a sampling of some unique moments in my life. My hope is that when you have finished the last page of my story, your journey to the island of Ormsö was worth the trip.

Contents:

A Little Bit of History   /11

Matchmaking   /14

A Bride Worth Her Weight in Whiskey   /19

Execution   /25

Axel and the Goose Chaser   /28

Country Store   /32

The Other Side of the Keyhole   /39

Bubbly Brown Soup   /42

Two Great Hunters   /47

The Eggs & I   /52

Mrs. Lou   /56

The Magic Water   /61

Club Fishing   /66

A Sled Full of Hope   /69

Angels   /77

Just in Time   /83

My Winged Skydiver   /86

Rudolf Linse   /96

The Foxhole   /107

Shield of Hay   /113

Graz   /121

Escape   /130

The Life Line   /134

Afterword   /142

*Our family in 1924.
Myself on Father's lap.*

A Little Bit of History

During the Viking Age at the end of the Eighth Century, many Scandinavians left their homelands to seek greener pastures. Some sought better tillable land to colonize; others were intent on conquest.

In the next two centuries the Vikings spread over much of Europe. On their route east, the Swedish Vikings crossed the Baltic Sea, passing by a small island close to the Estonian coast. This island, Ormsö, was a perfect stopover to re-supply and rest before traveling across land, then sailing the rivers into Russia.

Fragments from a Viking ship had been found deep in the mud of the island's largest lake, which connected to the sea. The saga told that Ormsö, literally translated "Snake Island" was named for a Viking Chieftain called *Långe Orm*, and thought that this ship in the mud belonged to *Långe Orm*.

The earliest recorded history of Ormsö was in the late 1200's when a great number of Swedes migrated eastward, with many colonizing on Estonia's west coast and the islands nearby. One of the most central settlement areas of the Swedes was Ormsö.

Since the Seventeenth Century, the island had been occupied by a succession of Swedish noblemen, the first being Baron Magnus Gabriel De la Gardies. He enlarged his holdings by a dramatic move. According to legend, during a wedding feast, the villagers were tricked into the sea where they disappeared. The Baron quickly moved to seize their land.

The next Baron, Otto Kristian Engelbrekt von Stackelberg, took over the estate and acquired more land for himself in the spring of 1764. When all the men of the village were out to sea fishing, the Baron's men drove the women and children from thirteen farms, altogether one hundred people. The farmers complained to the government of Estonia, but no action was taken. Instead, the Baron completely took over the land. In addition, he forbade the islanders to house any of the displaced hundreds. They were totally enslaved. *Salt-Simas* was among the farms that the Baron confiscated.

My great-great-great grandmother was a wet nurse for the von Stackelberg's grandson. It is not known why, but for her services she was gifted the farm, *Salt-Simas Gården*. Her husband was very likely the Captain of the Baron's ship, which brought salt from abroad, hence the name, *Salt-Simas*.

Generation after generation was born, with each ancestor being content to remain on the island to farm, fish and raise children. The Swedish-speaking settlers, here for over 700 years, left an imprint on the landscape and culture which was distinctive to Ormsö. The archaic dialect spoken was isolated from the mother country, and when an islander traveled to Sweden, was only partly understood to speakers of modern Swedish.

Houses were dirt-floored, and roofed with thatching, void of chimneys, causing the dwellers to devise special methods for venting during burning time.

Dress on the island was original to Ormsö. Women looked nearly identical, from the top of their head, hair parted in the middle, to their feet, clad with black homemade leather shoes, long straps woven around the ankle and half way up to the knee. The ever-present scarf, of a black, red and white pattern adorned every head. Black woolen dresses, skirted with half-inch wide pleats and black woolen jackets, buttoned from waist to neck completed the outfit. The village men were not as strict about their dress, and when they traveled to

Ormsö woman
Drawing by Pia Seffers

markets in Estonia and Sweden, they had the chance to see how other men were clothed, they adapted to the new styles.

On Ormsö, surnames were seldom used. The common custom was that each person was identified throughout the island by the name of their village, their farm and their given name. Everyone born on our farm was called *Fäll* after our village, *Fällarna* and our farm *Simas,* along with their first name.

Katarina Glad was my maternal grandmother. In her youth, she was hired to care for the children of Pastor Österbloom, a Swedish Baptist missionary sent to Ormsö. In 1886, when the missionary family returned to Sweden, they persuaded her to join them. Grandma had many suitors in Sweden, but feeling it was more important to be near her family, she returned to the island and married. She gave birth to five children, but only two survived, my mother Agneta and her sister, Katharina.

My story begins with *Fäll Simas Agneta*, my mother. Please let me introduce you.

Matchmakers

Agneta was reluctant to begin undressing. She fingered her blue linen dress that matched her deep blue eyes, wondering why her parents were so late.

At 11 p.m., the Swedish midsummer sun still hesitated to abandon the landscape. The white birch trunks bordering the meadows like pillars of a temple glowed in the Nordic night.

Agneta had placed lily-of-the-valley in a vase on her bedside table. The vase was made from a thick birch branch hollowed out by her father for her recent fourteenth birthday. She stared up at the ceiling, studying the knots in the uneven boards. Her parents had been gone an unusually long time. Had they gone out fishing with another couple in the Baltic Sea? Agneta knew that the barrel of salted smelt was getting low and Father rarely turned down an offer to go to sea.

The old grandfather clock in the next room ticked steadily. In an attempt to induce sleep, Agneta began counting the bells of the delicate flowers on her table, but losing track, she gave up.

The young swallows and field larks had stopped demanding food for the night. Everything on the farm was quiet. The cat crawled over the sleeping dog stretched out at the door and curled up in front of the wood stove, now cold during the summer.

Just as the sun dropped behind the trees, Agneta's heavy eyelids began to close. Then there was a sound. She sat up and turned her head towards the door. Footsteps. Her parents, Anders and Katarina, had come home. Knowing they would be unhappy if they knew she was still awake, she kept still.

Agneta could hear her father slipping off his boots at the stove, then propping them upside down on a rack to air. Her Mother opened the cupboard and pulled out the wooden bowls for breakfast, placing them on the table, while Father asked Mother for help to hang up a woolen blanket over the bedroom window. At this time of year, it was dark for only a few hours each night.

Usually, her parents didn't speak while readying for bed, but tonight Agneta heard their faint whispers. Quietly, she inched out through her door and tiptoed to her parent's bedroom door. She leaned against the wall and listened at the crack between the door hinges.

She heard her father say, "I just can't handle all the farm work alone anymore. We need a son-in-law. Agneta has to get married soon."

"Oh, no, Anders. She is too young," Katarina pleaded. "I haven't even been able to teach her how to weave properly yet."

"Don't forget, she'll stay right here, you can still teach her. Kärrslatt Hanas Johan, who we met tonight looked strong and grown-up to me."

"Are you thinking he would make a good husband for Agneta?"

"He could," Anders reasoned. "Next spring I'll need help with the plowing and seeding. The decision has to be made soon."

Agneta held her breath and sank down on her knees. On the island, she knew that finding a husband was not her decision. Marriages were arranged by parents, a custom unchanged for hundreds of years. The luxury of falling in love was a distant hope for a young girl. Even though her father had no sons to help him on the farm, just two daughters, Agneta mistakenly thought her marriage would be in the more distant future.

Agneta stumbled away from the door and ran to her room, slumping on the bed. Her thoughts shrank to a few sentences, repeated over and over. Who is he? What does he look like? Tears fell on her clenched pillow. I don't know how to be a wife, she thought. Would he even be willing to have me? Maybe I'm not pretty enough for him.

After a few hours of restless sleep, Agneta arose early to wait for her beloved Grandmother Maria, a feisty woman known for her independent thinking. Agneta crawled out through her open window and sat on the long bench outside the main door. She waited for Grandma, knowing she would soon arise and prepare for milking the cows in the far pasture. The milk pail clanged on the door as Grandma slipped to the outside.

"What's wrong, Agneta?" Grandma asked, gently stroking her granddaughter's hair. "Didn't you sleep well?"

"I slept a little," Agneta replied, then whispered, "I have a secret." Agneta took Grandma's gnarled hand and led her away from the house.

They paused at the gate. "What is your secret, my girl?"

Agneta hesitated. "Grandma, you have to promise not to tell."

"I promise," Grandma vowed, lifting her hand as a pledge.

"Mother and Father have decided I should be married! I overheard them last night. They have already found a young man for me."

"Who?"

"He's from the neighboring village. His name is Johan Lindström, from the farm called *Hanasa*. Do you know who he is?"

Grandma wrinkled her forehead, "I don't know him, but I know the family. They are a respected family. I think there are two sons, Johan is the youngest, about seventeen."

According to the custom, the oldest son or daughter stayed on the farm and inherited the property. Johan, being the youngest, had to be matched with a daughter who would inherit her farm. This was Agneta.

"But Grandma, I have to see him. Now," she pleaded.

"Wait a minute. Let's figure this out. I have heard that the Lindströms are building a stable. Your young man will be helping," Grandma said.

As the two approached the pasture, Grandma Maria instructed that Agneta should first milk her two cows as usual.

"Can I go then?" Agneta begged.

"Yes. If you hide in the juniper bushes nearby, you can spy on your intended without being seen," Grandma suggested.

Agneta agreed to the plan, then Grandma gave directions to the Lindström farm.

As soon as Agneta finished milking her cow, she gathered her long golden hair into a knot behind her neck and ran, determined to avoid anyone on her way. It wouldn't do for a young girl to be seen spying on a young man.

Her bare legs moved as fast as the spokes on their hay wagon on the narrow, uneven road leading to the neighbor village. Short of breath and red faced, she often stopped to listen. No, she couldn't hear any hammers or saws. She was still too far from the village.

After running a little farther, she found the road turning off to the right and leading to the farm where Johan lived. Agneta stopped to listen. The house and its surroundings that Grandma had described must not be too far from the juniper grove, Agneta reasoned, and walked carefully closer. Was that hammering? Did someone holler?

Agneta dove into the soft moss covered ground, with her heart hammering like the hammers not far away. Well shielded by dense undergrowth, she crawled closer to the working men. Between the tall junipers, she saw a building larger than she had ever seen before. The six sunburned men, bare backs shining from sweat, worked as they talked loudly to each other.

In an effort to keep calm and study each man one by one, Agneta sprawled on the ground and rested her chin in her sweaty palms. She concluded that only three of the men were in their late teens. But which one was Johan? Then she heard someone call out his name, Johan answered, and for the first time, Agneta laid eyes on her future husband.

He's very handsome and quick she thought to herself, a little on the short side. But throwing that thought aside, she took one last look, removed the stick of juniper branch she had been chewing on, and crept silently out of the woods. Her feet moved faster yet on her return to where Grandma eagerly waited, sitting on a stump with the milk buckets at her feet.

At the moment Agneta saw Grandma, she hollered, "I saw him! I saw him! He's handsome, he's quick and strong!"

"My dear granddaughter, calm down. Your parents are probably only looking around trying to find a good match for you. We don't know anything about if and when. You are still too young and maybe so is he."

"But Grandma, I'm sure I heard Father tell Mother he needs help on our farm soon."

"Listen, my dear. What you heard in the middle of the night through a crack in the door could be different from what your Father really said and meant. They didn't say anything about when they might arrange a meeting. At this moment, we don't know what their plans are."

"Grandma, you mean they are not going to say anything to anybody for a long time?"

"Well, dear, we just have to be patient. All you and I can do now is pray and wait."

Within a few months, the match had been arranged. Both sets of parents agreed on the dowry, chose the wedding date and supervised the couple's first meeting.

A Bride Worth her Weight in Whiskey

"Guarding the Gate" was a custom practiced on the island. Centuries ago, groups of Vikings were plunderers, taking advantage of farmers by charging a toll to pass through a gate leading to the market.

Presently, in 1906, those not invited to a wedding carried on this tradition by blocking the gate to the bride's farmhouse. These "guards" would not allow the wedding party to pass until a "toll" had been paid. The amount of the "toll", usually 100 proof Swedish *aquavit*, was determined by the bride's attributes, her dowry and her inheritance. Agneta's dowry was a farm with orchards and livestock. And, she was pretty.

Two men, Oscar and Nils, were in charge of guarding the gate to the bride's home. Bundled in homespun woolen clothing, they swung their arms to keep warm, mimicking the blades from the three village windmills, standing in a row in the nearby field.

"They should have been here an hour ago," Nils thundered. Like an ancient Viking, six feet tall, he fixed his stare on the empty roadway.

"If we don't hear the sled bells from the sleds soon, we'll send out a search party. In this heavy snow and deep drifts, anything could have happened. Or they might have stayed in the church to wait out the storm," Oscar reasoned.

Nils shrugged his shoulders and with some difficulty, reached deep in his chest pocket and pulled out a bottle of rum. He maneuvered the bottle between the icicles formed on his bushy red beard and drank deeply. Having approved of its strength and quality, he passed the bottle to Oscar.

While the gatekeepers stood guard at the gate to *Salt-Simas Gården*, Agneta and Johan waited impatiently at the church for the pastor to arrive. The white stucco church, built in 1219, was cold. The cast iron heater in the corner seemed to struggle in its effort to warm the room. Dozens of wedding guests circled the stove, stomping their feet in an attempt to keep warm, while singing folk songs to relieve the tension.

The bride and groom, Fäll Simas Agneta and Kärrslätt Hanas Johan, were urged into the center of the crowd, and there, received warmth from the stove as well as from the singing guests.

The best man, Kärrslätt Jobas Anders, stepped through the thick of the crowd and walked towards Agneta and Johan. One of the best man's duties was to offer a gratuity for the pastor's services which in those days was a bottle of liquor.

Ander's voice was deep and his manner kind, but with a shade of concern he turned to the bridegroom and whispered, "I'm worried about the pastor. He should have been here an hour ago. I gave him the customary two liter bottle two days ago."

"Two days ago?" Johan blurted.

"I guess I should have waited until today, but I felt sorry for him living alone in his parsonage. Do you think he might have….?"

Like a military commander, the bridegroom ordered, "Take Nysimas-Lars and look for the pastor. You must find him!"

Agneta drew close to Johan and whispered, "Is anything wrong with the pastor?"

"I don't know. We'll soon find out. Regardless, we are going to be married before we leave this church," Johan answered.

The bride had no more questions. She hung firmly on to her future husband's hand. The sparkle in her eyes and the smile on her face affirmed her acceptance of the uncertainties in life. She shifted her grip from his hand to his strong arm.

The bride's sister, Katharina, impatiently flung her shawl around her shoulders and dashed out into the snow. When she peeked around the far corner of the church, she jumped back. "Oh, no."

There, steadied by Anders and Lars, the pastor staggered towards the church. Katharina swung around and rushed back into the building, straight to her sister and stammered, "Pastor is stumbling, but they're coming, they're coming!"

Once inside, the pastor shuffled up the aisle, leaning heavily on Anders. His silver cross swung from side to side on his chest like a pendulum. Anders deposited him squarely behind the carved pulpit and the ceremony began. The best man reached for his violin and the music echoed through the centuries' old church.

Trying to suppress a yawn, the pastor faltered over a few words, then, resolutely, he focused on his task and proceeded with the liturgy, ending with the pronouncement that Johan and Agneta were now husband and wife. The guests dashed to surround them with congratulatory hugs and handshakes and followed them out to the waiting sleds.

Johan put his new bride in the sled, and tucked her into her woven blankets.

Agneta turned her face towards Johan, and whispered, "What about the gatekeepers?" Anxiously she dared to ask, "Do you have whiskey?"

"No," the bridegroom answered. "But don't worry. Tonight we will sleep in our own bed."

Agneta shivered. She leaned back, bit her lip, but remained quiet. Johan saw that her cheeks had turned as red as apples, which reminded him of the apples on the trees at the entrance to her farmhouse. He gripped his bride tightly and kissed her.

The wedding party waited in their sleds for a sign to depart. Anders stood up in his sled, waved his fur hat and the horses and sleds charged forward through the snow.

Johan's spirited horse bolted in an attempt to overtake the lead sled. Agneta remembered what her father had said about Johan's skill in choosing and raising horses. She turned wistfully for one last look at the church.

Johan's stallion reared up and snorted steam through his nostrils. His black mane flurried about the bells around his curved neck. The travelers sped on the road, over fields and through thick forests, racing towards the newlywed's farmhouse, where the couple would face their first challenge; the men at the gate.

After traveling an hour, they reached the field surrounding Agneta's village. In the distance, they saw plumes of smoke curling skyward from her family's chimney. Deep in thought, Johan whistled quietly, while his mind silently worked out his strategy to avoid the guards at the gate.

At the gate Oscar suddenly shouted, "The bells. I hear the sled bells."

The arrival of the bridal party was imminent. At the approach of the wedding sleds, the gatekeepers shifted their positions, sizing up their opponents.

Nils ordered, "Hold your ground," and stepped up on the rungs of the gate, while the rest of the men took their stance.

A hundred yards from the gate, the wedding party gathered and Father gave instructions. With reckless abandon, the best man charged his horse and sled to the gate, but in the last moment halted abruptly, causing the sled to swing around and ram the gate squarely in front of the guardsmen.

Stunned, they scattered, hollering at each other to shore up the perimeter.

Close behind, Johan's vibrating animal reared up on his hind legs. He turned the horse to the right and away from the gate.

Aiming for the spot where the months-old snowdrifts had hardened and reached the top of the fence, he told Agneta, "Hold on, we're going to crash over the fence!"

The animal exploded and charged over the fence, black mane flying and snow swirling up to his flanks. A splintering and cracking of the time-worn fence was mixed with cries and shouts. The entire wedding party and sleds followed, coming to a sliding halt in front of the porch, where guests excitedly watched the drama at the gate.

A hush engulfed the porch, broken only by the tinkling sled bells, as Johan placed the traditional crown on his bride's head. In one swift movement, Johan scooped Agneta into his arms and proudly carried her over the threshold to the cheers of family and friends.

Both sets of parents rushed to the couple and pulled them to the dining tables, covered with a white linen cloth trimmed in red, which had been placed in a U-shape for the occasion. Johan and Agneta were seated at the head of the table, while others took their places at the two extensions. Behind the bridal couple, the wall was hung with white sheets and decorated with fir branches. The table was laden with plates piled high with smoked ham, jellied meats, potatoes, and rice. Fruit soup and white bread ended the feast. Completing the festive meal was homemade beer, or *mjöd*, supplied by the bride's family.

Kärrslätt Jobas Anders was called upon to play his accordion while couples danced until nearly midnight. Johan and

Bridal Attire early 1900's
Drawing by Pia Seffers

Agneta were anxious to be alone, and soon the guests began making their way out into the cold night.

In the next few months, the couple settled into the routine of the little farm, sharing the small house with Agneta's parents. Johan proved to be a great help to his father-in-law, especially learning the secrets to growing fine fruit trees. Agneta busied herself with learning the techniques of dying wool for weaving. Evenings were quiet, except for the thump- thump from the loom where Agneta's mother kept a watchful eye on her as she practiced weaving, learning the patterns her mother used, which she herself would use in the future. The men sharpened tools by oil lamplight, and always ended the evening with Bible reading.

The next year, with joy, sixteen-year-old Agneta and eighteen-year-old Johan welcomed their first child, a boy. With this arrival, the farmhouse was becoming increasingly crowded. Johan and Agneta were anxious to have their own place. Between the farm work, Johan and his father-in-law cut timber to use for a new farmhouse for the young couple. Johan was intent on a more modern house than his in-laws. The Missionary Österblom, for whom Agneta's Grandma Maria worked, had introduced to the island the advantages of having a chimney, a "luxury" the islander's stubbornly avoided in the past. By the time the third child arrived, the farmhouse was finished and the young family packed their belongings and moved into their own farmhouse 50 yards away.

Execution

Although country after country occupied Estonia and its islands from the 12th Century on, Ormsö would always remain entirely Swedish, both in culture and language.

Estonia had been part of the Russian Empire until the latter part of WWI when Estonia proclaimed its independence. The Russians were reluctant to leave as agreed upon, and began to vandalize and harass the Estonian people. The Estonian government had no choice but to take matters into their own hands.

Swiftly, men between the ages of 18 and 39 were drafted into the newly formed Estonian army. After only a few weeks of military training, they were pronounced ready to face the enemy. Since Estonia was administratively in charge of Ormsö, this draft extended to us.

With a wife and now five small children to care for, Johan did not respond when the draft order came in the spring. If he were forced to leave the farm to join the Estonian army, there would be no one to plow and no one to sow. Having no other income than from what the farm provided, Johan stubbornly made the decision to ignore the draft call, even under threat of the firing squad.

A few weeks later however, Johan was arrested and taken across the bay to Hapsal, Estonia and imprisoned. The penalty for his defiance was indeed the firing squad.

Agneta was devastated. The children gathered around her, crying and questioning why their father didn't come home. After a long sleepless night, Agneta made her decision. Her determination outweighed her fright. She must get Johan back home, whatever the cost.

Early the next morning she left the children in her mother's care and crossed the bay to stay with a friend in Hapsal. She spent the entire night on her knees praying, pleading with God to save her husband.

In the morning Agneta felt at peace. She walked to the converted military headquarters and resolutely walked into the building.

The narrow waiting room was crowded with parents and wives of young men who had dodged the draft. They all hoped for a miracle for their loved ones.

Agneta saw the Lieutenant in charge looking out a small window in his office door and scanning the waiting room. He stared dispassionately at the families huddled together for strength, but when his face turned towards Agneta, his eyes froze in horror. She was frightened by his reaction. They had never met. What did it mean?

Just then her thoughts were interrupted when a woman in uniform came from the end of the hall and announced to three mothers waiting that their sons had been executed yesterday. Wailing and disbelief filled the room. Forgetting her own fears, Agneta reached out to give what comfort she could as the families slowly emptied the room.

Before Agneta could return to her seat, the door swung open and the Lieutenant motioned for her to enter his office.

Agneta was unable to suppress her sobs, trembling. The Lieutenant pointed to an overstuffed chair in front of his desk, but at first she hesitated. He then turned from her and walked slowly to his desk. Agneta slumped into the chair, clutching Johan's picture to her bosom, while dabbing her wet eyes with a linen handkerchief.

Abruptly, the young officer stood and faced her.

Agneta searched his eyes. Should she speak?

"I….I prayed all night," she sobbed.

The Lieutenant turned away and paced the floor with his eyes downcast, while Agneta waited anxiously for him to speak.

"You appeared in my dream last night," he spoke at last. Then faintly, "Just as you are sitting before me now. You were crying and small children were trying to comfort you."

Agneta's voice caught as she lifted her hope filled eyes. "I was in your dream?"

The man circled his desk, fingering the pistol hanging from his belt.

Haltingly he began. "Yes, all night your face tormented me. I agonized over the meaning. Until I saw you in the hallway I didn't understand the significance of my dream. Now I do."

He took a deep breath. "Tonight your children shall have their father home."

Agneta struggled for a moment to fully grasp his words, to look into his eyes, but he turned away, escaping his emotions.

Then with a military salute, he dismissed her.

Agneta thanked God for His mercy and rushed out through the door to await her freed husband.

Axel and The Goose Chaser

Sounds of axes, hammers and saws woke me up out of a deep sleep. Next to me in the straw bed, my brother Lars-Eric snored, completely unfazed by the loud racket outside.

I carefully stepped over him down onto the cold wooden floor. Curious about the noise, I ran out to the front porch where Grandma sat on the bench, finishing a new pair of shoes.

If Grandma Katarina wasn't cooking, baking or bringing in wood and water, she was knitting and telling us children stories from by-gone times. Exciting stories, often about her life as a youngster. Sitting at her feet, our eyes were glued to her face as each dramatic story unfolded. We never tired of hearing the stories, even after dozens of times.

Grandma, at four feet, eleven inches and barely 100 pounds, seldom walked, she raced. Her feet moved in such a way that you wondered if they really touched the ground. Her white apron-covered dress, with yards of flying fabric, could easily hide two or three of us younger children. We children knew she would always step in to defend us from the spanking rod. Her long white skirts then became our fortress, a place where we felt safe.

Often after the rest of the family went to bed for the night, I would sneak into the kitchen and find Grandma mending socks, reading her worn Bible or just sitting quietly, rocking in her rocking chair. I sometimes wondered if she ever slept. With so many grandchildren, there were always small ones to hold in her arms. Her humble smile and red cheeks, shining as two red cherries, were well known on the island. Mother and Grandma made all of our clothing. Mother sat at the loom for hours, weaving shirts, blankets, virtually everything.

Grandma's specialty was leather shoes, which she taught each of us boys to make. She sat weaving a strip of leather through holes in the upper edge, gathering the hide to fit snugly around an ankle. Noticing me, she called.

"Come here and try these on, Axel," she said.

As Grandma fitted the shoes on my feet, I looked up and saw my father and two of our neighbors at the open well. The two men were pulling the long jagged saw back and forth across a log, helping Father to replace the rotten upright post for the crossbar to rest on, a device used to pull up water from the well.

Wells were built up on a knoll, and whenever practical, situated close to the house. Even though there was a five-foot square frame with a lid covering the rock-lined shaft, the well needed to be thoroughly cleaned once a year. During cleaning time, a man was lowered by rope to the bottom of the well, usually twenty to thirty feet, where he would scoop the water into buckets for emptying up at the surface. After the water was emptied, this man would scrub the bottom with a hand-made birch brush until clean.

I tugged on my knee length shirt typically worn by toddlers, and stared at our five geese grazing on the field between the house and the well. I had always been afraid of the geese with their terrifying hissing and flapping wings, their beaks threatening to nip at my toes and yank at my shirt. The rest of my family spent most of the day in the fields, but I, being too young to help, was often left at home with nothing to do. I longed to explore the farm, to watch the "naked" shiny piglets roll in the mud, or bring carrots to the baby long-legged horse. I giggled when he searched for my fingers to suck. But the geese were forever at my heels, taunting me, holding me prisoner, it seemed. I was terrified to leave the porch.

I stared once again at the geese, hoping the men working at the well would be a distraction, so I could run from Grandma's protection across the field to Father.

The early morning sun felt warm but I shivered in fear. The white geese were only a few feet away from the porch where I stood at the top step.

Then, as if on command, all five suddenly swiveled their heads away from me. Here was my chance. I seized an empty milk bucket for protection and flung myself off the porch, catapulting into the soft grass. Taken by surprise, the geese hesitated just long enough for me to dash across the field into my father's arms.

The two neighbors sat on the big log next to the well taking a break. Father set me down on the log beside them and headed towards the barn. Just as I began to tell the neighbors how mean the geese were to me, the big gander lowered his head to the ground and charged at the log where we sat. The man nearest scooped me up to safety on his knee and screamed at the geese to go away.

Father was chuckling at the sight as he came from the barn. From behind his back, he brought out an odd looking contraption. It didn't look like a farm tool or anything I had seen before.

"What is it, Father?"

The two neighbors gathered around him, curious about this gadget.

Father's mustache quivered as a smile emerged when he handed the object to me. I studied the long stick, then the wheel at the end, which was nailed sideways to the stick. Father had attached a narrow strip of shiny tin against the uneven surface of the wheel.

"Son, this is your 'goose chaser'."

"My 'goose chaser'? How do I use it?" I asked.

Father showed me how to hold the stick, push the wheel on the ground, and when I did, the wheel rotated, making a terrible clatter. Father gently shoved me towards the curious geese who stood warily on guard nearby. "Go on, run after them."

I took his cue, thrust out my chest and galloped head long into the middle of the flock. The geese scattered in all directions, honking and flapping their wings and stretching their long necks high up into the air. Emboldened, I chased after them through the fruit orchard, not caring that I trampled the newly planted gooseberry bushes, past the hay barn and down the hill to the pond.

Quacking furiously in defiance, they hit the water hard, and I slid on the wet grass to within inches of the pond. I hooted, and the geese turned their long necks towards me in unison, staring with their black eyes.

I lifted my new goose chaser triumphantly over my head and whooped for joy.

I sprawled at the edge of the pond, absorbed by my new power. The tension flowed out of my small body. The geese quieted down and dipped their heads into the brackish water, pulling and picking at grass and bugs.

After a short rest, I gathered my new device and ran back to the farmyard where I found Father still at work on the well, balancing the crossbar.

Chattering about my adventure, I told him how the geese had shrunk in fear and how glad I was that now I could go unescorted to the barn, no longer a victim of a pack of silly geese.

Father and I sat down on the porch steps and Grandma brought a tray with the lunch she had saved for me. How good the smoked meat and hardtack tasted. After lunch, I wrapped my goose chaser in an old blanket and tenderly placed it under my bed.

Sleep came quickly, but not before I hugged Father in thanks for my goose chaser, my doorway to freedom.

Country Store

Early in the morning one sunny spring day, I looked out the window to see Father at the buggy. I rushed outside and tugged on his coat, "Are you going somewhere, Father?" I asked.

"No, your mother is going to the store to buy some sugar, also some needles for Grandma. She plans to visit her sister, Katharina if there's time," Father informed me.

Noticing that I was clad only in a shirt barely covering my navel button, Father told me to go back to bed. I passed Mother coming out the front door.

"Axel, why are you up so early?"

"Mother, please, I want to go to the store with you. I'll be good, I promise. If you take me, I'll weed your vegetable garden everyday. I'll sweep the floor and feed the chickens. Please, Mother?"

"No, Axel. Look at you. You're dirty all over and your clothes are torn. You'd better go back to bed now. A four-year old needs more sleep. Another time I will take you to the store. In the meantime, your clothing must be repaired."

With six children still at home, the mending and sewing was a monumental task limited to her spare time, of which there was little.

Mother had just removed seven loaves of rye bread from the enormous brick oven. Often in the winter before the oven cooled completely, I would crawl through the opening and fall asleep surrounded by the warmth. But today, I went back to my bed of straw in my room. But no sleep came. From the window I saw Mother preparing to wash her hair at the open well across the yard. I knew it would take a little time to complete her task and Father would not return from the pasture with our horse just yet.

Barefoot, I sneaked outside again and wandered over to the buggy. I fingered the blue blanket covering the seat. It was so pretty, with a dark blue background, and covered with stripes. Mother had just finished weaving it the day before.

My older brothers and sisters had told me so much about the store, bigger than our barn, with shelves full of things they hadn't seen before. I could almost smell the sticky red peppermint candy piled up in a giant bowl on the counter. I imagined the smell of paint that Father bought for the barn and visualized the wooden rocking horse my brother told me about. Oh, how I would love to see it all. But since Mother needed to travel to the island's only store just a few times a year, my chances for accompanying her were limited.

I stroked the wool blanket again. My eyes darted from the barn to the house, then with one quick leap, I landed in the buggy and crawled into the hay and under the blanket just before my father returned from the pasture.

He harnessed our brown mare, Flicka to the carriage, helped Mother into the seat in front, and handing the reins to her said, "The young horse is high spirited today. Be careful. Try to be back before dark."

"I'll try, but you know I haven't visited Katharina in a long time."

Mother jerked the reins and Flicka sprinted through the front gate. At the edges of the blanket where the sunshine trickled through, I studied the poppy seeds, small bugs and the occasional ant embedded in the sweet hay. The buggy swayed gently as my eyelids began to feel heavy. I slept on and off.

It seemed like hours before the horse and buggy jolted to a stop. Peeking from under the edge of the blanket, I saw Mother grab the feed sack and hang it from the horse's neck, then hurry into the store. My heart pounded and my stomach cramped. Do I dare climb out and sneak in? No, I'd better wait for Mother to return.

I wanted to lift the blanket again to see the children I could hear playing around the store. Carefully, I eased up one corner. Three girls in bright dresses chased two boys. Just when one of the boys came close to our buggy, I sneezed.

"Somebody's under here," he yelled. All four of them came running.

As if summoned by the commotion, Mother swung open the shop door and ran to the buggy. She quickly shooed the children away, then, with one grand swoop, ripped the blanket off.

She hissed between her teeth. "I should have known, Axel," she said harshly. "Don't move."

I whined, "I just wanted to see the store. Please Mother, just through the door?"

"No. Just look at you. You are dirty, uncombed, no pants," she chided, shaking her head. "And that short shirt!"

She grasped the railing of the buggy and I felt her hot breath and smelled the familiar scent from the juniper stick she chewed on, mostly when angry. With a flurry, she leaped into the front seat and yanked the reins. Chickens picking in the dirt cackled and scattered as we sped away in a cloud of dust. Agonizing about my fate at the end of our journey, the trip became the longest of my life.

At last, I felt the buggy slowing and wondered if we had reached home. But when we stopped, it was my Aunt Katharina's kind voice I heard, welcoming Mother to her home.

She must have noticed the anger on her sister's face, "Oh, Agneta, you are upset."

"I am. Look!" With a jerk, Mother threw the blanket to the ground. "Many piglets that I have taken to the market have been cleaner than this one. Have you ever seen such a dirty sight?"

I hung my head at Mother's sharp words. At that moment, I wished I had stayed home.

With hands firmly placed on her round stomach, Katharina exploded in a loud laugh, "Oh, how sweet you are, Axel."

Tenderly, she lifted me out and carried me straight to the wash basin outside and plunged me into the tepid water. She scrubbed me from head to toe, laughing all the while. Finally, she wrapped me in a towel and set me on an outside bench to dry in the sun.

Turning to my mother, she chuckled, "Isn't he an armful of sunshine? I wish one of my two girls had been a boy."

Mother burst, "Well, maybe I'll just let you have him."

The two women settled down at the table for coffee and after an hour of gossip, Mother decided it was time to head home. But Aunt Katharina announced she had a plan, and whispering, unfolded it to Mother.

Aunt Katharina scooped me up and placed me on the dining room table. "We'll get you into the store yet, Axel."

Both sisters suppressed laughter as they scattered colorful pieces of clothing all over the table. I dropped my head and looked down. Confused, I stared at all the garments, wondering at the black leather shoes and long white stockings, and the white funny-looking hat.

"Let's try this one," Aunt Katharina said, pulling a red and yellow garment with white collar over my head.

I felt detached and my thoughts were firmly fixed on the store. My mouth watered just thinking about all the candy I might soon taste.

Finally, Aunt Katharina announced, "Perfect!"

She lifted me down from the table and guided me to the mirror. "You are ready for the store."

My eyes grew large as I stared at the mirror. In disbelief, I touched the colorful clothes, from the collar down to the hem. I fingered the long ruffled sleeve cuff and bent down to pick at the bowed shoes pinching my toes. My hands fell dead to my sides.

The boy in the mirror was a girl!

I closed my eyes, blinked them open again and sighed.

The figure looking back at me was still dressed like a girl.

With a cry, I dove into Aunt Katharina's ample pleated skirt and sobbed, "But Aunt, I don't want to be a girl!" Seizing the hat from my head, I hurled it to the floor.

Placing her hands on my shoulders, she said, "Axel, you'll always be my special boy."

I tried to squirm from her arms, but she led me gently to the awaiting buggy. "Your Mother and I are going to the store, and you're going too."

Mother thrust me down at the rear of the wagon. I grabbed a handful of straw and bit hard, muffling my cries.

Aunt Katharina soothed, "The store is full of so many wonderful things." With a wink, she pressed two small coins into my palm.

Arriving at the store, Mother tied up the horse to the post. I held the coins tightly in my fist and climbed down, tripping over the hem of the long dress. Hiding behind Aunt Katharina's wide pleated skirt, I entered the store.

My Aunt's face lit up when she spotted the shoe corner and soon shoes were piled high on the counter. Mother stepped briskly to the fabric counter in the far corner where she pulled out bolts of plaids and laces, draping them across her shoulders, stretching and stroking each one.

Watching the two from behind the flour barrel, I spied an open door. I squirreled into the room and shut the door. On a shelf close to the floor, a row of stuffed bears welcomed me. In a wink, I hid behind them and dozed off.

Sometime later, with a high-buttoned shoe dangling in her hand, Katharina asked Agneta anxiously, "Where is Axel?"

"I thought he was with you, Katharina." Both sisters dropped their merchandise and began searching. "I'll check the buggy," Mother suggested, "and you search the store." Moments later Mother returned empty handed.

"No sign of him," Aunt Katharina exclaimed. "What are we going to do? Let's ask the storekeeper for help."

After they explained their problem, the man inquired, "Have you looked everywhere?" Biting on his long yellow pencil, he thought for a moment, "Come with me."

The storekeeper stopped in front of a red and green door decorated with a picture of a rooster. The door was locked. He scratched his head, "I am sure I left this door open a little while ago."

He pulled a bundle of keys from his pocket and unlocked the door. The tiny storeroom was lined with shelves completely covering the walls. The lower shelves were inhabited by flour and sugar sacks, and step by step the shelves became narrower where smaller items were stored.

For several minutes the sisters scanned the room.

"No Axel anywhere," Katharina proclaimed.

"Wait…what was that?" Mother hesitated. "I'm sure I heard something. Listen. It sounds like Axel whispering in his sleep like he often does at home."

She tiptoed towards the sound, pushed a bear aside, and there, on the lowest shelf behind a huge polar bear I slept, still clasping the coins firmly in my hand.

Mother fell on her knees and swept me into her arms. "You scared us, Axel. Why did you run away?"

Fully awake now, I sobbed, "Look at me! Everyone thinks I'm a girl. I don't want to be a girl!" Big tears ran down my cheeks.

"Please don't cry," Mother cooed, wiping my face with the hem of her dress. "Look what I have for you." She held up a pair of wool pants and brown canvas shoes.

"Oh, Mother," I exclaimed, tearing at the dress. "You're not mad at me anymore?"

Mother shook her head and held me tightly. "I can't be mad at a boy who risked being laughed at just to gain a peek at the store."

Reaching into her pocket, she presented me with a warm gingerbread cookie studded with raisins.

I dove into the new pants and with a scream of delight rushed out of the storeroom, colliding with a tall man. Slowly lifting my head, I timidly looked at his broad smile. "I came to see the store, sir."

"You are invited. Let me show you around."

I was overjoyed to be back in Mother's good graces again. I could almost endure being dressed as a girl, but the disapproval of Mother I couldn't bear. I looked back at her. A loving smile filled her face, "Go ahead, Axel, enjoy the store."

The Other Side of the Keyhole

Today was Sunday. Sunday schools were held in private homes, one in each of the fourteen villages. Since my father was the Sunday school teacher in our village, classes were held in the living room of our farmhouse.

I brushed my long flaxen hair to the side and peeked through the keyhole. Wanting to make sure that I was alone in the hallway, I looked to both ends of the corridor, and satisfied, put my right eye up against the hole once again. Through the opening, I saw the children from our village filling the room. I dug my fists further into my pockets. My cheeks grew hot. Maybe this Sunday Father would allow me to join them. I thought I should remind him that I would be six years old next month.

Just then, I heard Father enter the house from feeding the horses. I eased the kitchen door open and heard him making lather from pieces of soap in a wooden bowl of hot water. Father sharpened his large razor knife on his belt and then I heard the scraping as he moved the knife over his beard. As long as I could hear the knife in action, I felt safe at the keyhole.

For as long as I could remember, I had wanted to join Father's Sunday school class. You need to grow a little more, Father always said.

Through the hole I saw the children dressed in their Sunday finest. The girls sat reverently, but the boys stood on the narrow benches behind them, chattering and throwing spitballs. A couple of boys didn't seem any older than I was. From where I peered, I could see the open door to our courtyard where some children were still wiping snow off their feet on fir branches at the threshold.

I saw Karin, whose brown hair covered her forehead like a curtain. Britta wore a woolen dress with a linen cord around her waist. The two sat down together, dangling their feet back and forth as they read from a thin gray book. I knew what they were doing. They were memorizing Bible verses to recite for Father. The older girls sat quietly in another row, whispering to each other.

I thought they were all having so much fun, just being together. Why couldn't I join in? I had watched from behind the same door every Sunday, always hoping that I could be a part of the class.

This Sunday I had made up my mind. I would convince Father that I was old enough to enter Sunday class. The more children in the class, the better, I reasoned. I knew how to read my Bible.

The scraping of Father's whiskers stopped. Quickly, I moved away from the keyhole. Father came into the hallway, glancing at me, his youngest son. Father's highly polished shoes gleamed under his Sunday black suit. A scent of the pine soap still lingered in the air. Father looked so dignified and handsome.

"I know the same verses by heart as my sister Maria," I whispered boldly.

Maria, my only sister, was fourteen. My three older brothers had already moved to mainland Sweden. Maria often took care of me like a second mother, taking me berry picking, or even fishing in the nearby lake, both enjoying the nature around our farm. On longer trips, she brought a basket filled with pancakes and a bottle of milk. It was a special treat to mix the freshly picked blueberries with the milk. I always seemed to be hungry.

Father's hand gripped the doorknob. This was my only chance.

I pulled Father away from the door, "May I recite, Father?"

Father hesitated, but nodded, "Let me hear you then."

My eyes sparkled. Without hesitation, I recited two of my favorite Bible verses. Father looked pleased.

"May I be allowed to join in, Father?"

"Yes," Father said, his eyes crinkling. "I can see you have studied your Bible well and want to please God. It is time to come to Sunday school."

Father and I stepped into the room. The children stood up respectfully. Their eyes turned towards us, and the smiles on each face warmed me like the sunshine coming in through the window. I walked straight and proud and took a seat on a bench behind Maria. She winked at me. Karin tousled my hair and handed me her songbook.

Father took his place on a chair at the front of the class, close to the fireplace where the burning logs crackled. All the children quieted, preparing for the day's lesson.

Overwhelmed with a sense of belonging, I bowed my head and joined in the opening prayer.

Bubbly Brown Soup

During the summer, we were anxious to taste the sweetness of the first strawberries of the summer. My older sister, Maria, made the jelly every year and as soon as the berries began to ripen, she was up and out of the house early to reap the harvest.

"Your sister and brother went berry picking at sunrise and they might be home before Father and I," Mother informed me.

She sat on the bench weaving at the loom. I was lying on the floor under the loom, helping her by handing up the requested threads. "All right, Axel. We're done for today."

I helped Mother cover the loom with an old sheet to protect it from the dust.

"Don't forget to feed the piglets and bring in the eggs," she instructed. Without so much as a backward glance, Mother threw her shawl around her shoulders, left the house and stepped into the awaiting buggy. Father grabbed the reins and they were gone.

Silence. From every corner of the house, silence seemed to close in on me. I was alone. On our island, it was not unusual to leave children as young as seven alone during the day, but today I felt especially deserted.

Dragging my feet as slowly as the 101 year-old in the neighboring village, I plopped down at the kitchen table and stared out the window. Watching a spider weaving a silvery dew-covered web outside the kitchen windows, I yawned.

Was that a knock at the front door? Very faint at first, then a little louder. I slipped to the back of the house, startling my yellow cat sleeping in front of the door. Quiet as a shadow, I sneaked outside around to the gable of the house.

At the rose bush, I crawled on all fours and peeked around the corner, then sighed with relief when I saw my friend, Fäll Klosas Edwin, at the front door. I whistled. Edwin pressed his body close to the door to avoid the rotten apples I threw at him from behind the roses.

"I know it's you, Axel. Stop it!"

I didn't answer. Instead, I ran around the house to the other gable and crouched behind a water barrel. Edwin threw a rock at the barrel. With a shriek, I flew through the air and grabbed my friend's shirt collar. His left hand flung towards the sky and his right hand flipped across his heart, our secret code for surrender. Now laughing, we held a short conference about what to do next.

"OK. How about going down to the lake and see what's going on there?" I suggested.

"It's too hot," Edwin complained. "Let's go to our cellar instead and cool off. We can eat some pears left over from last year."

Both barefooted and dressed in white homemade shirts barely covering our knees, we ran across the field separating our two farmhouses.

To reach the inner cellar, we had to go through an outer door, down the dirt walkway, then through a smaller door. The stone-floored cellar was small and dark, lit only by the sunlight entering the open door. The room was lined with shelves full of jars of pears and cherries and on the bench lay a basket of brown eggs. I walked over to the far corner to investigate what we might eat, when I heard a strange noise.

"Listen. What is that bubbling sound?" I asked.

"Oh, it's just something in those wooden bowls on the upper shelf," Edwin answered, pointing.

"What's in them? Why are they bubbling?"

"It's an after dinner treat for the grown ups. After it has bubbled for a few days they eat it like soup," my friend tried to explain.

Staring at the shelf, I blurted out, "Can we taste just a little?"

Edwin stepped on a bench and stretched up on his toes, fetching two wooden spoons and a pine bowl. We sat down on the foot high threshold and Edwin placed the bowl between us.

Gingerly, I licked the liquid, then swallowed the contents of the wooden spoon filled with the brown soup.

"Oh, it tastes good." I was eager for the next spoonful. "How do they make it?"

"It's supposed to be a secret," Edwin whispered. "I don't know if I should say. Promise you won't tell anyone?"

"I promise," I replied.

"One day I hid behind that big barrel there in the corner and watched my father fill the bowls with several scoops of the brown water from the round wooden tub. Mother put several slices of toasted rye bread and three spoons of sugar in each of the bowls. Days later it was ready to eat."

"But the bubbles….where do the bubbles come from?"

"I don't know. But it sure tastes good."

Licking the bowl I asked, "Can we have another one?"

Edwin placed another bowl between us. Soon, that bowl was empty too.

Then, all of a sudden, I felt quite strange. I snickered, "Look Edwin. My spoon is crazy. It's rolling around in my hand. Do you see it? It moves by itself! Here come the bowls too!"

"I'm going to fight them off," he laughed and tried to pull the spoon from my hand.

I swung around and held my long spoon up in the air like a sword and gestured to Edwin to fight. But then, something came over me.

I cried, "The floor is spinning. It's going to hit me!"

I slumped to my knees and crawled up the dirt walkway and over the threshold. Looking up, I saw Edwin down on his hands and knees too. We stumbled outside. The tall green grass just beyond the threshold turned brown as we emptied our complaining stomachs and lay sprawled in a stupor.

I lost track of time. I had no memory of making the trip home, yet when I awoke I was in my bedroom, curled up like a ball on the floor. The room was dark and hot, cold sweat dripped from my forehead, soaking my long white shirt. I heard footsteps coming towards my room. I managed to drag myself up on the bed and pull the sheet over my head.

The door opened slowly. I heard Mother whisper to Father, "He's asleep."

My head was spinning. I tried to tame my wild thoughts. How did I get into this bed? Why is my green stool dancing on the floor? I was petrified when I thought I saw the table in the corner jump up and down, jerking in unison with my throbbing temples.

I heard our front door open and the loud voice of Edwin's mother, "Good morning, Agneta. I'm worried. This morning, Edwin didn't want to get out of bed and felt sick to his stomach. He claimed he spent all day with Axel playing around the house."

The two mothers continued to talk, but now in a whisper. I couldn't understand a word they said. My heart pounded and my stomach cramped. In my battle to calm my spinning head, I finally sunk into a deep sleep, escaping my misery.

Sometime later I heard Mother. "Are you still asleep, Axel?" She gently pulled the sheet off me and placed her cold comforting hand on my burning forehead and leaned forward to kiss my cheek. Somehow, I managed to sit up.

"Are you sick?" Mother asked.

I had to escape Mother's questions. "I've got to do my chores," I stammered, throwing back the quilt and setting my feet on the cold floor.

Out through the back door I flew and stumbled towards the corral, barely finding my way to where the hungry sheep awaited in the pen. I released them into the pasture, then inched my way to the chicken house to collect eggs. When I staggered back to the house, Mother was busy in the kitchen. As I passed, she put her arms around my shoulders.

"Sit down, Axel. Tell me the truth. What happened yesterday?"

"I'm not sure," I stuttered, twisting on the wooden stool. "Everyone left me alone. I was scared. Then Edwin came. It was so hot outside. He said we could cool off in their cellar."

"What happened then?" Mother prompted, eyeing me with sympathy.

"Edwin and I found some wooden bowls filled with bubbly brown soup."

"And you ate it," Mother filled in.

"Yes, we emptied two of them."

"Two of them? How could you?"

"But grown-ups eat it, Edwin told me." I squeezed my hands between my knees to stop the shaking.

"You could have killed yourself. That wasn't soup," she said emphatically. "It was homemade alcohol!"

"Alcohol? Am I going to die?"

Mother reassured me, "No. No."

"I'm never going to have alcohol again in my whole life. Never!"

My stomach began to rumble. I hastily kissed Mother, burst out the door to hang my head in the gooseberry bushes behind the house. As I emptied my stomach, I repeated to myself, "Never again! Never again!"

I heard Father and Mother chuckling. Maybe tomorrow I would laugh about it too, but of one thing I was certain. No more bubbly brown soup for me!

Two Great Hunters

Not a winter passed without snow covering the whole island, thawing only at the end of March or beginning of April. A foot of snow had fallen during the night, our first big snow of the season. Instead of warming ourselves inside by the fire, we preferred to take advantage of the snow, sledding or skiing.

I giggled as I pushed my older brother, Lars-Edvin off the porch causing him to land head first into the deep fluffy snow. He quickly jumped back up on his feet, and grabbed a nearby shovel, heaving a load of snow at me, but I ducked just in time.

"Here comes Father!" Lars shouted, hearing the squeaky barn door open.

Quickly, I picked up some fir branches and helped Lars brush the snow off his coat. As Father neared us, he looked upward at the sky, probably trying to determine the chances of more snow.

"Are you boys dressed warm enough?"

"Yes, Father," we answered.

Both of us wore red woolen caps pulled down over our ears. Heavy long scarves reached from our necks to our waist, partially covering our sweaters and wool pants. Our woolen stockings, stuffed into a pair of homemade shoes were pulled up to our knees. We looked eagerly into Father's face as he stepped closer. His cheeks burned red from the cold.

"Boys, I want you to go out to our timberland and look for browned fir trees and mark them for firewood. Mark them with these," he said, pulling strips of narrow multi-colored fabric from his pocket and giving them to Lars-Edvin. From his other pocket, Father retrieved a half dozen fresh biscuits and handed them to us.

"I expect you home before dark." Pausing, he added, "The snow is deep and there could be more on the way before nightfall."

My toes felt cold already and my nose was running. I was anxious to get moving to warm up.

"Mark at least fifteen trees. Axel can stand on your shoulders, Lars, and mark them as high as he can reach."

Father pushed his fur cap high above his forehead and said, "I hope to sell them in town for firewood just before Christmas. Also mark a seven-footer for our Christmas tree. Put a red piece of fabric on the top of the one you choose. If we get heavy snowfalls, we'll need the markers to find the trees."

With an encouraging clap on our shoulders, he wished us well.

The early Saturday morning air was crisp and still, and the sun lingered behind the distant woods. With every step we took, the snow crunched under our feet. I trailed in my brother's tracks, thankful that he forged the way. Foxes had been tracking alongside the fence and many small bird tracks zig-zagged. From the tracks, we could tell that the fox had taken long leaps in pursuit of his prey. Lars pointed to numerous tracks typical of the large Nordic hare. During the day, the hare would usually hide in a crest of a snowdrift or knoll. When disturbed, he escaped by long leaps, almost like a kangaroo.

Suddenly, Lars stopped. He whispered excitedly, "Look! Those tracks running alongside that wooden fence are huge."

I bent down and studied the footprints. "It must be a big male out foraging for last summer's growth of willow trees."

"Come on, let's see if the tracks go through the fence to the other side. I know the hare never jumps over a fence. They have to find an opening large enough to crawl through," my brother explained.

We scampered alongside the rickety old wooden fence. Where the fence made a turn up the hill towards the woods, we found a gaping hole. We knelt and looked at the tracks and the opening in the fence.

"Let's track him down, Axel. Maybe we can catch him. The sun is high and it must be close to noon, so first we'd better mark the trees for Father."

Lars bent down in front of the first tree while I stepped up on his back, then his shoulders.

"Hold still!" I complained. "You sway like a rowboat in bad weather. Can't you get closer to the tree?"

"Can't you see I'm sinking?" Lars grumbled.

Father had told us it was hard work, but after tumbling so many times off Lars' shoulders, I wondered if his unsteadiness was intentional, for he seemed to take great pleasure in digging me out.

My brother must have forgotten our constant companion, hunger. I complained to him, "Can't we eat some of those biscuits now?"

"Let's see how many trees we have left to mark." He pulled the colored strips from his pocket and counted. "Five more trees. I guess we can afford to take a break now."

We climbed up on a big stump and sat in the sun eating. "Wouldn't it be nice if we could eat these special biscuits every day?" I sighed.

Lars nodded in agreement, as we washed them down with snow.

"Let's hurry now and finish marking," Lars said.

We marked the remaining trees and set about making plans to catch the hare. On the island, hunting was not for sport, but rather out of necessity, to supplement our meager diet. We had learned about hare hunting from Father. The knowledge of the ways of animals in their own habitat had been handed down for generations and Father was well versed in animal behavior. He had an aversion to guns, so he devised an ingenious method to catch different animals during the snowy winters.

Lars and I remembered how Father had explained his system for catching hare. The hunter would determine where the hare might be hiding during the day by the tracking pattern. From the position of this grouping of tracks, one could suppose the hare to be in a particular area. This area we would circle trying to figure out the most likely spot where the hare would sleep. We knew the hare would only be awake during the dark hours.

Lars and I split up, each taking a part of the circle to explore, noting the number of tracks leading into the middle of the circle and how many led out. We ringed the area until we agreed that the hare was in fact where we suspected, inside our circle. From the appearance of the vegetation and traces of bark and willow shoots freshly gnawed, we could be fairly certain the hare tracks were recent.

If the snow was deep and new-fallen as it was now, the hare goes into hiding for several days. Father had told us if we could get as close as possible without walking directly on where he is hiding, he would most likely just lay still. Then we should approach the hiding place and throw a piercing scream into the cold air. The frenzied hare would eject from the hole, stunned and unable to move for a second or two, just the amount of time needed to grab him.

"Do you think it will work?" I squealed.

"Sure it will. Let's hurry."

We dashed to the stump where we had found the first "in" track and started to count the "in" and "out" tracks.

I pointed out, "See how he has jumped from here over the top of the stump."

We figured out a wide circle several hundred feet in diameter. We left the stump in the opposite direction wading through the deep snow, hustling through underbrush, across flat-top hills and climbing over fallen trees, each counting our "ins" and "outs" and keeping in eye contact as we worked on our own half of the circle. Finding more "in" than "out" tracks, we then walked a smaller circle around the meadow with the knoll in the middle until we determined he was still inside the circle.

We scanned the rest of the circle and suddenly Lars tensed and whispered, "I'm sure he's lying in that deep snow drift next to that bush."

The plan was to approach him from both sides and on Lars' signal, leap and scream as loud as we could.

In the stillness, we could hear our own heartbeats. As we crouched, slowly approaching our target, Lars' arm suddenly flew up. We leaped and screamed. Nothing happened. Disappointed, we took a closer look and discovered that the tracks were several hours old.

"It will be dark soon, we have to leave for home now," Lars-Edvin said, exhausted.

The setting sun illuminated the landscape with brilliant colors, but in our disappointment, we barely noticed it. With long, dragging strides, Lars moved on. With each step, I got further behind. The sun disappeared behind tall pines at the top of the next hill. Home seemed so far away. I realized I needed to catch up with Lars. I tried to run, but I fell. The snow was too deep.

Then I saw it. The hare.

I jumped to my feet. A giant white hare flashed in front of me. My screams echoed into the woods.

The hare somersaulted. I leaped at him and threw my arms around his quivering warm body. We tumbled over and over in the snow. I was surprised at the size and strength of the animal. Lars rushed over to me and grabbed the hare's legs. We tied his lanky, now limp legs together with rope. What a fine specimen he was.

I hoisted the fluffy bundle on my back like a rucksack and we started for home. My mouth began to water just thinking about the tender rabbit meat bubbling and simmering in Grandma's cast iron pot. But more than that, we were already reveling in the praise that would be heaped on us for catching the first hare of the season.

The eggs and I

Christmas celebrations were over and as soon as the new year had slipped through the door, our family began to talk of the much longed-for spring. Week by week we could sense the subtle changes in the weather, when the snow began to convert its pale face into thousands of tiny streams. Spring, my favorite time of year, brought warmth and light back to the winter-darkened Nordic landscape. The trees, flowers and hibernating animals were awakening at every turn.

Every spring my enthusiasm always focused on the large duck, the merganser. The males were black and white with a touch of green mixed into their black head feathers; the females were gray with reddish-brown heads and necks. I had been studying them for years.

Tree holes excavated by woodpeckers were the duck's preferred nesting homes. I worried about them this year because one by one, rotting trees had been cut down for firewood, or simply to thin the forests, forcing the ducks to make their nests in unsafe places, like dilapidated hay storage sheds too close to the ground. Foxes and weasels had snatched eggs and occasionally a grown duck from the nest.

After a winter of dried fish and home-canned food, Mother became increasingly frustrated with ways to feed the family. We anxiously looked forward to the time when our chickens would be laying eggs again. We missed the cookies, pancakes and many of the other dishes that required a treasured egg or two. On occasion, Mother would use a duck egg, and when mixed with other ingredients, tasted nearly the same to us.

An idea popped into my head. I would try to save the mergansers by providing nests and also start a business collecting and selling duck eggs. I asked Father to save all the lumber scraps for me and when I had gathered enough materials, Father and I built ten breeding boxes. When each was finished, I covered the bottom with a few inches of hay and sawdust. By March, all the boxes were done and Father and I set about to nail them in the trees. To make the ducks feel safe, I climbed high up in the birch and alder, some 20-25 feet. Father tossed a rope up to me, strung the box on the rope and I pulled it up, then nailed it sturdy to the tree trunk.

In the meadow below our house and to the east, the trees were spaced far enough apart to allow the big ducks to circle between them. After the boxes were up, each day I would watch from the kitchen window, anxious to see if any ducks would be curious about the box and move in. One morning, I saw a pair fly in circles 100 to 200 feet away from the box. The big ducks flew in pairs, male and female side by side, so close it was a wonder they didn't hit each other's wings. Suddenly the female flew in the direction of the house the pair had chosen, slowed, then she dove into the box. Satisfied, the male flew away alone.

All the pairs seemed to use this method of selecting a house. So complete was their acceptance of my boxes, that they did not even supplement the bedding. Later in the spring, when the female flew unescorted, I knew she was incubating. I was thrilled to see that all ten boxes were "rented".

I told Mother of my plan to sell duck eggs on the mainland to help out our family. But she reminded me that most people would probably think the taste too "wild". Since our family really had no preference from chicken to duck egg, she suggested that I ask Father if I could sell chicken eggs instead.

When he agreed, every two weeks or so I would gather the eggs in my basket and travel on the ferry across the bay to Hapsal to sell our eggs at the open market. In only a few hours, my eggs were sold and I returned home. Mother was anxious for me to supply her with duck eggs, but of course, I couldn't just go to a nest and take all of the eggs. The ducks would then abandon the nest. I had to devise a way to prevent this.

By trial and error and simple logic, I found that I could remove one egg if there were four in the nest. I would mark an entry on my ledger, then two days later, I would check the nest again and mark my list. If the "renter' had laid additional eggs, I could perhaps take two. I always made sure to leave enough eggs so that the mother would not suspect my strategy. Over the course of two months, I was usually able to collect between 40 and 50 eggs from each nest, leaving eight to ten eggs behind. After a time, when I noticed that the ducks had spread enough fluffy down over the eggs indicating that it was time to incubate, my business of removing more eggs from that nest was over.

One day, I watched one mother duck throw her little ones out of the nest down to the ground. She seemed to count them by lightly pecking each one on their fluffy backs. Satisfied with her brood, she turned towards the lake, uttered a harsh "karrrr, karrr", then turned to be certain that each tiny duckling followed in a single line. They were probably heading for the Baltic Sea less than a mile beyond the lake.

I so looked forward to next spring when these ducklings might return to the parents' former home, which I had so carefully and lovingly made. I was very proud of my accomplishment in bringing home badly needed coins for the family, but even more so, happy that my ducks now had their own families.

At the kitchen table one morning, I was bent over my ledger, adding and subtracting figures on a page. My sister Maria, who had just returned home from mainland Estonia where she had been enrolled in a one year modern housekeeping course, entered the room fumbling with her apron strings behind her back.

"What are you doing, Axel?"

"I'm just keeping track of my ten "renters," I answered

Maria laughed, "Your renters? They're just ducks, Axel." With that, she swung around to the stove and began breaking kindling into small pieces for a fire. Soon the stove was hot enough for her to begin making the very thin Swedish pancakes we loved so much.

Unruffled by Maria's comments, I returned to my ledger, adding the number of eggs every "renter" had laid, and how many I had removed during the entire season.

Some hours later, Maria called me outside, pointing for me to sit on a bench near the barn.

"Axel, I need your help. Tomorrow, we have a guest coming from mainland Sweden and I am going to be responsible for our dinner. We have nothing to eat as the main dish." A shadow crossed her face. "I asked Father if I could have a chicken or two but he said no."

Puzzled, I wondered why she was telling all this to me. If Father had said no about the chickens, Maria would just have to figure something else out.

Maria took a deep, long breath, "Axel, I need one of your ducks."

Stunned, I shook my head. Did I hear her right?

She repeated, "You'll have to give up one of your ducks."

I mumbled, "Those ducks are my renters and they have paid in full.'

"Axel........."

"No, Maria. Hear me out. What about all the dreams of the mother, about her little ones growing up, having fun, nesting themselves some day?" How could I make Maria understand? I was intimate with the merganser's family, their routines, their very lives. Maria was asking the impossible.

Maria's eyes softened, but never left mine. Perhaps she sensed that nothing she could utter would soften the blow she had dealt to my very heart. Then slowly she went inside without saying another word.

Alone, I remained on the bench until the sun was gone. The chill from the night air met the chill from inside me. I was sickened to the very core of my being. My tears flowed, hot and fast.

I sat for a long time, wrestling with my thoughts.

Bit by bit, the moon came up over the tree line.

I thought of our guest.

Then I walked into the dark woods towards the duck houses.

Mrs. Lou

One night at dusk, I rode Flicka to the west end of the island near the Saxby Lighthouse, searching for objects that often washed up on the shore. In the dim light, I saw shadows prowling. Smugglers, I wondered? After WWI, there was a lack of products imported into Estonia, and because the import taxes were so high, smuggling became a lucrative business. Ormsö was used as a stopover for the smugglers, so the Coast Guard's duty was to confiscate the smugglers' cargo and report their activities to the authorities on the mainland.

I waited. Step by step, in the loose sand they came, closer and closer. My mouth went dry. Then I saw a dog. Yes, it was Lou, and with her, two guardsmen on late patrol. The guard crew on our island consisted of only two men. Patrolling the coastline on foot was the norm, but in an emergency, they could seize one of the numerous fishing vessels to take chase.

The old lighthouse was used as an outpost in the 1930's by the Estonian Coastguard, who kept a close watch over the waters to the west from our island.

One of the young men, Toivo always had a ready smile. He was the favorite of us children. He remembered our names and knew which village we came from. The older man acted as if we were in his way. But we tolerated him because he was teamed with Toivo. Their green uniforms and caps, adorned with shiny emblems and insignia engaged our fascination.

But the real object of our affection was Toivo's dog, a huge German shepherd. Her soft fluffy tail wagged incessantly and if we didn't pay attention, she would lick our faces profusely. The dog loved to play, tumbling and nudging us to the ground.

When we first met Toivo, I asked for the dog's name. The proud owner hoisted his slender six-foot body straight and boasted, "Mrs. Lou."

"Is that really her name, sir?" I asked. "I've never heard that name for a dog."

"Aren't you about nine years old? You should have learned about America by now," he replied. "Lou is the First Lady, the wife of President Hoover of America, the strongest country in the world."

He commanded Lou to lie down in our midst and directed, "Lou, show them what the First Lady does when the President is visiting another country."

The dog dropped her head and whined a mournful cry. The crowd broke into spasms of laughter, while some children rolled on the ground, trying to imitate her.

The two guards and their families lived a mile and a half south of our village, in a cottage next to the abandoned estate from feudal times, Magnushof. Beginning in 1748, in succession, this "castle" was inhabited by German barons who had enslaved the farmers to work on their estates, even seizing the farm animals.

In 1890, the farmers joined together in an uprising, burning, looting and killing some of their oppressors. The fourteen-room, two story building was destroyed, but the stables, and the brick long building with its double stone walls were still standing and useable. It was in this long building that the guards and their families now lived.

Toivo often came to visit my family. He knew that he and Mrs. Lou were welcome on our farm and in our village. We had one of the larger orchards on the island and Father was always happy to share his produce with friends and neighbors. He liked to favor the two coast guard families, who so often were in need of food and other supplies since their pay did not stretch far enough.

In those days, it was difficult to serve as a guard. My Father told me that the two men had little time to make many friends. The bitter cold and ice during fall and winter were their worst enemies. Spring had its own risks for the guards, when the ice started to become brittle and the threat of drowning became real.

One afternoon in early spring Father brought home sad news.

"Son," he said, "your friend, Toivo, has been in an accident. He fell through the ice. Apparently his dog had tried to pull him to safety, but couldn't. When people heard her loud barking, they rushed to the scene to help. But by then, he had been in the icy water too long a time. Your friend is very sick."

When Father saw tears in my eyes he said, "Don't cry, he is in the hospital now. After supper tonight our family will pray for his recovery."

For the next two days and nights I barely slept, crying every time I thought about him or when someone mentioned his name.

During those days, Father often put his arm gently around me, while I asked over and over, "If Toivo dies, will we meet him in Heaven?"

Father replied, "Of course, son. We will all meet there."

The next few days were long and dark. My Father went to the only phone in the village and telephoned my oldest brother who was a schoolteacher on the mainland close to the hospital. Father found out the young man was indeed very sick with bronchial pneumonia. The next few days just crawled by as we waited anxiously for more news.

Then the dreaded call came. Toivo had died. I felt numb. Our entire house was in mourning.

"Why? Why did he die?" I pleaded with Father. "Couldn't God help him?"

Father looked at me and I saw tears in his eyes. When he answered, his lips quivered, "Son, maybe God needed him more than we."

The next morning, Father and I filled a basket with apples that we had preserved in hay through the winter, as well as newly baked bread to offer to Toivo's widow. Our visit was short. We had no words of real comfort.

Father hugged her and I held her hand while looking at a motionless Mrs. Lou under the table. Her bushy tail and beautiful head were limp.

Not even my offering of a piece of bread could move her.

Saying goodbye, Father told the young woman that she would be welcome at our home anytime.

"And bring Lou too," I added.

Showing our love for both of them was a poor substitute for her husband we realized, but it was all we could do.

During the next few months, the widow and Lou visited us quite often. With fall approaching, jobs became scarce on the island, and after the mourning period was over, Toivo's widow decided she had no choice but to leave her home and start a new life on the mainland. A few days before her departure, she visited us with Lou at her side.

We all sat down at our table while Mother served coffee and her delicious cardamon bread and jam. Lou sat at my feet under the table, gulping the small bits I gave her. The widow thanked mother for her kindness and stood up to leave.

"I don't know what I'm going to do with the dog. She doesn't seem to want to leave the island. She's still looking for her master. At times it seems that she expects him to walk back into the house," she added, tears rolling down her pale cheeks.

Father and I stood quietly.

After a long pause, she collected herself and said, "You seem to be the only ones on the island that she really cares for. She loves to play with your children."

Lou stood close to me. I wanted to grab her collar and not let her go, but waited for Father to say something.

I looked at him, wanting to cry out, "We'll keep her," hoping he would offer to keep the dog.

The widow looked expectantly from Father to me. "I don't know if I can earn enough to feed her."

She wrapped her black shawl around her head and started to walk away, calling for Lou to follow. But the dog remained at my side.

"Can't we keep her, Father?" I sobbed.

"We're already feeding seven children, son."

"But Father, I'll dig in the ground for potatoes we missed. I'll pick our cherries and trade with the neighbors for meat bones, or bread, or anything, I'll do anything," I rattled.

The widow stopped at the gate. Her eyes fixed on me. She waited.

I grabbed Father's sleeve in desperation. I must make him understand how precious Lou was to me.

I cried, "I can always find scraps from the annual slaughtering in the village and mix them with mashed potatoes."

Father didn't seem to hear my pleadings. He grabbed the dog by the collar and with a swift, determined stride, caught up with the widow. I bit my lip.

Father's back was towards me and I couldn't hear their words, but my heart sank.

I waited for Toivo's widow to walk through the gate with the dog.

But instead, I heard Father say, "Yes, we'll keep Lou."

Tears of joy welled in my eyes when I realized that Mrs. Lou was to be mine.

From then on, we were inseparable. I hoped that somehow Toivo would know that Lou was in good hands.

The Magic Water

It was near midnight. Eerie shadows from the tall pines criss-crossed the cemetery. In front of me stood the old church, built in 1219.

I dismounted my horse, Flicka, then we made our way to the undertaker's holding cottage. I paused to recall the incident of a few hours ago that led to my reason for being here in these ghostly surroundings.

I was brushing Lou's long silky fur in the late afternoon when I heard my sister, Maria, sobbing. She stood at the long outdoor bench, yanking a brush through her brown hair, and frowning at her image in a piece of broken mirror.

"What are you doing, Maria?" I asked.

She whirled around and I saw tears running down her cheeks.

"I am invited to a wedding in the next village tomorrow as a bridesmaid. My hair just won't behave. One side is limp and the other flies all over my head. I only have until noon tomorrow. What am I going to do?"

Just then, our white-haired grandma appeared from around a corner of the house, joining us at the bench. Grandma took but one look at my sister, put her arms around her and reasoned, "Forget about your hair at the moment. Take this milk bucket instead and milk the last two cows in the pasture farthest away. I have already milked three cows and I'm tired. When you get back, pour the milk into the buckets in the basement. And then, it will be time for bed. Don't worry about your hair. I'll help you fix it tomorrow in good time for the wedding."

Maria seemed relieved and went willingly in the direction of the pasture. As soon as she had left, Grandma grabbed my shirttail, pulling me down on the bench beside her.

"Axel, young man," she said, "tonight you are going on an important mission." Grandma continued, her mischievous blue eyes piercing mine. "You are a brave young man, I know. Remember when you and your dog Lou chased away a whole band of teenagers trying to let your rabbits loose?"

"Yes, I remember."

I tried to catch what she was leading up to, but she ignored my confused expression. By experience, I knew Grandma was up to something. She had her own ideas how to solve problems, often frustrating my mother with her unconventional ways. Her unbelievable toughness and physical strength became especially clear one spring day at dawn. A neighbor's heifer had repeatedly broken into Grandma's vegetable garden, damaging her crops. She first tried to repair the fence, but had little success. Next she reminded the neighbor, Erkors Lars, of his duty to repair his portion. He ignored her pleas again and again.

One day, Grandma decided to take matters into her own hands. She hid behind a large juniper close to the broken down section of fence. As the cow broke through, Grandma raised a heavy fence post and struck the young cow behind the shoulders with all her might. With a thud, the heifer crashed to the ground. When Erkors Lars discovered the heifer, he came to our farm to ask Father if he had seen anything unusual concerning the heifer. We all wondered what had happened, but no one had an explanation. Grandma kept this incident to herself for many years.

"Axel, get your horse."

Mindful of Grandma's persuasive powers, I ran to the pasture, where Flicka met me at the gate. As she munched on the piece of bread I had brought, I slipped the bridle over her ears, swung up on her back, and galloped back to Grandma, who patiently waited for me on the trail.

Grandma revealed the secret mission. She and I were often conspirators, but never before had I played such an important role in one of her schemes. She handed me my rucksack, then prayed to ask our Heavenly Father to protect and lead me.

She stroked Flicka's neck and calmly whispered in her ear, "You are a good horse. Don't fail your master tonight."

Through undergrowth, between thickets of trees, over a swamp, we charged, avoiding the main roads. Our journey was dangerous. Flicka stumbled numerous times, but managed to keep her balance. Low branches caught at my clothes, but I hung on. The horse slowed when she felt I was gliding too freely on her back.

Sooner than expected, I saw our goal up ahead, the ancient cemetery. It was nearing midnight and in spite of the late hour, the Nordic midsummer sky gave us enough light to see the way.

Flicka seemed to understand that we must conquer the steep, sandy bank leading to the old church, surrounded by the graveyard. She surged powerfully and we shot halfway up the bank, sand flying all around us. Without warning, at mid hill, we faltered. My skin went cold under the cover of sweat. Flicka quivered under me like the beginnings of an earthquake. As we wheeled around, we both fell, gliding down sideways. A sudden stop against a stump gave us time to recuperate. I knew my horse would fair better if I gave her free reins.

In moments, Flicka rose to her feet and we ascended again. Using a different approach, I applied gentle pressure with my knees to her sides, alternating right and left. She responded by zig-zagging up the bank and we reached the top.

The bright full moon now hovered over the treetops, and the tall pines shadowed us. A short distance away, the stucco church appeared majestic. I felt at ease in spite of the graves with black iron crosses surrounding us, like soldiers on guard.

In the centuries' old graveyard, I began looking for the undertaker's holding cottage. During daylight, the sun reflected brightly off the roof of the cottage, for it was the only roof on the island covered with sheets of copper. Now nearing midnight, with the brightness gone, only my memory of the exact location guided me.

I followed the gravel path as it wound around the cemetery. There it was. At the two corners of one gable stood two wooden barrels, filled with rainwater.

Grandma had told me that the barrels contained "magic" water. Legend was that rainwater collected at midnight from a copper roof would turn dull hair into glittering gold.

With Flicka at my heels, I stepped carefully towards one of the barrels, and just as I filled my two containers, the church bell loudly tolled twelve. I threw my rucksack with its treasure on my back and mounted.

Turning away from the old cottage, I froze. I thought the old cemetery would be eternally quiet, but the night was abruptly filled with a high shrill pitch. It sounded to me like swords clashing on shields, as though the Vikings of old had come out of their graves and were in battle. I spun around in time to see that it was only the red foxes quarreling near the cottage.

Menacing shadows surrounded me, and I closed my eyes. I knew my horse would find her way out of this dark place better than I would. I gave her free reins again.

As we passed familiar meadows, swamps and trees towards home, my senses began to return. Back on familiar ground, I was in control. As the

St. Olai Church on Ormsö

distance from the cemetery increased, I felt calmer.

Drenched with sweat, my tired horse and I longed for rest. Lou greeted me with yelps and barks as we reached our farmhouse. I hid the precious water in a safe spot near the sauna and dove into a pile of new mown hay nearby and fell instantly into a deep sleep.

Early the next morning, I awoke at the sound of my sister Maria fetching water out of the well. I rubbed sleep from my eyes and picked hay from my hair. What was I doing in the hay? Slowly, I recalled bits and pieces of the night before.

Just then I heard Maria's voice. I stumbled over to the bench where she was preparing to wash her hair.

"Dump that water on the roses, Maria."

"What?"

"Close your eyes," I ordered and ran to recover the containers from the hiding place and held them behind my back.

"Axel, what are you hiding there?" Maria insisted.

"Oh, nothing much. Just a little "magic" water for your hair."

Proudly I handed the two containers filled with magic water to Maria. She dropped her hands to her sides and just stared at me.

"What makes it "magic"?"

"Well, remember the copper roof at the cemetery.......?" I hinted.

Maria's eyes widened and her mouth dropped open. "You braved the cemetery at night just to bring me the "magic" copper rainwater for my hair?"

"Sure, it was just a short midnight ride."

"Oh, Axel, my angel," Maria squealed, throwing her arms around me. She grabbed the containers and ran into the house and I headed to my room for more sleep.

That afternoon as I sat at the kitchen table carving a wooden horse, Maria burst into the house and planted a kiss on my check. She presented me with a piece of wedding cake she had saved.

"Thanks to you, little brother, I felt almost as beautiful as the bride!"

Club Fishing

The mountainous snowdrifts still lingered between the red and white Swedish farm buildings. Home early from school that April day, Lars-Edvin and I had spent hours sledding.

Hungry for new adventures, Lars suggested, "Let's go see if the pikes are running up the creek yet."

I agreed. From the barn we fetched two clubs made from thick wild junipers, where at the end, a knot of bulbous roots formed. The clubs were used in the spring to kill poisonous snakes found while haying, and also used for ice fishing.

My father told us that some years ago, the two-foot pikes had attacked people who tried to catch them by hand in the shallow creek. Their huge jaws filled with sharp teeth could almost reach around a human leg.

For two miles we dodged the snow piles and waded through wetlands, marked by clumps of alder trees and willows. We felt our faces burn from the sun and spring wind.

We finally reached the narrow creek and stood side by side at the edge. A score of feet away, we saw a rippling wake traveling towards us. Hypnotized, we stared into the clear shallow water. The dark green outline of a huge fish appeared, with its long white-bellied body weaving from side to side, then it disappeared into the shallows.

"Keep quiet," Lars whispered, as we crouched down on our knees to plan our attack.

Trembling with excitement, Lars sputtered, "Quick! Run down the stream to the bend where the creek narrows. We need a blockade so the fish can't get away."

I rushed downstream, gathering branches, rocks and roots to block the creek temporarily. In the bottom of the creek, I anchored branches and debris with more rocks forming a barrier. I returned upstream sweaty and exhausted.

"Look, Lars! A pike is speeding downstream towards you," I hollered. "A big one!"

Lars-Edvin leaped out of the water just as the angry pike snapped for his leg. The water churned as the fish whipped around into the hollows of a willow tree, its roots spread wide in the stream. We froze. Our eyes transfixed on the long "monster" lurking between the submerged roots. We watched the pike, it seemed to grow bigger as it slithered towards us. The creature's dull black eyes were mesmerizing. Trembling, Lars-Edvin lifted the heavy club slowly into position. The pike's jaws, lined with jagged teeth, opened wide as the stalking fish feverishly gulped water.

Bang! Lars hit the pike's head squarely with the club. The shallow waves cleared. All was still. The huge white belly surfaced, motionless. Lars hauled in his catch.

After hours of roaming up and down the creek, I thought I saw another rippling wake further upstream. Mixed with bundles of roots something greenish yellow appeared close to the surface. When I saw the outline of the fish, I shouted to Lars, "This one is mine."

The fish was shielded by roots. I tried to chase it out into the middle of the stream by beating with my club around the stump. Water splashed all around, hitting me in the face. Another bang. I swung the club over and over until the water became so murky that I couldn't see anything. Where did it go?

We ran downstream watching the surface for ripples. Nothing. We tracked back to the roots where the pike had hidden before. We had to find it soon, for dusk was approaching. On our knees we crawled close to the tree and peeked under the roots.

"Look!" Lars whispered, pointing to a shadow in the water. "It's the pike."

The knotted roots protected it like a cage. Clubbing would not work. Back home, before we left, I had sharpened the other end of my club to a fine point and now my success depended upon it.

The "monster" was within reach. But to catch the fish, I must pin it with my spear either to the bottom of the creek, or against a root.

I aimed and my spear broad-sided the pike, pinning it tightly against a clump of roots while Lars-Edvin struck a numbing blow on the side of its head. I scooted the pike up on dry land, just at the turn of the creek. The battle was over.

Dangling from a heavy willow branch, the two fish glittered in the fading sunshine. Singing an ancient Viking ballad taught to us by Grandma, we proudly began our journey home with our spoil.

Meeting us on the porch, Father cried out, "Either of you hurt?"

"No, only the fish," I answered proudly. "We just scooped them up out of the creek below the church."

Father stepped closer and took a good look at our catch. "This is going to taste splendid tonight after only salted herring since fall."

I sat down on the steps, exhausted, clutching my catch.

Father eased down beside us. "I don't think I've ever seen such big pikes. I'm proud of you, boys. Let's show Mother."

When I slipped into my straw bed that night my stomach still bulged from the feast. Content, we fell asleep quickly, remembering the praise Father had heaped on us.

A Sled Full of Hope

One evening in the winter of my thirteenth year, Father proposed a challenge that I would face the next morning. After explaining my mission, he sent me to bed early. My night was filled with dreams of horses and sleds in deep snow with ice breaking beneath the runners. Then, between dreams and wakefulness, I heard Father's voice, and the pop and crackle of fire from the kitchen stove.

"It's 3:30, Axel," Father's voice vibrated through the cold of the room. "Time to get up."

I hesitated. The two quilts covering my nest in the thick straw mattress felt too cozy to abandon.

Father's words hit my ears again, this time strong and followed by the word, "Now."

I jumped out of my bed and ran to the window. Oh no. Several inches of new snow had fallen on the already thick blanket. The temperature remained at several degrees below zero, but the sky was clearing, a good sign.

My thoughts rushed in all directions. Are there going to be other thirteen-year olds traveling with the sled train? The task of taking goods to market on the mainland was often given to young sons, testing their budding manhood.

How difficult will it be to sell a whole load of firewood in town, I wondered? Hunger was our big family's constant companion during the harsh winter on this tiny island. Ormsö's soil was rocky and unsuited for productive farming. Only potatoes and rye could be harvested with some success on our farm. Meat was scarce and other crops failed to thrive, making for hard times nearly every winter.

In front of the hot stove, I yanked on two pairs of woolen stockings, followed by two pairs of heavy pants, topping this with a knitted wool undershirt, heavy sweater and parka. I shivered, more from my anticipation of adventure than from the coldness of the room.

Our narrow driveway was barely visible after the night's snowfall. I knew the main road would be in better condition, compacted from the horses and sleds that had already passed.

My heart pounded as I jumped into the pile of hay in the forefront of the sled lined with a large lambskin. I felt like a soldier plunging down into a tank, ready for action. Up on my knees, I reached for the reins.

"Axel, I expect you to do a man's job," Father announced, handing me the reins. All I saw from under Father's fur hat were his iced eyebrows.

"I'll do my best, Father," I replied and squared my shoulders.

In a cloud of snow, Flicka plunged ahead instinctively, stepping powerfully to prevent the sled from stalling. Father had distributed the load well, allowing Flicka to manage with confidence. She pranced down the last hill and I steered her in a wide arc, sliding to a stop behind the last awaiting sled.

I watched the sled-master stop at each sled, rechecking harnesses and loads. Flicka restlessly threw her head up and sideways.

Just then, the tall slender sled-master approached my sled.

"Are you alone?" he asked.

"Yes, sir. Just Flicka and me," I answered.

"You're the youngest one joining the train today," he said, patting my shoulder. "Call on me if you have trouble. It could be a difficult journey today. Clouds are forming in the west. Well, keep warm," he said, and returned to his place at the head of the train.

Steam arose from horses and men, and was gently carried away by the morning breeze.

Our sled-train began to crawl along the nine-mile road, picking up several more sleds with travelers before reaching the ice covered bay. An additional dozen travelers had joined our train, all heavily loaded with varying merchandise. Many were loaded with firewood, or apples packed in hay or smoked and frozen fish stacked like firewood. Food staples such as sugar and salt, and occasionally nails or iron bars had to be purchased, so the farmers brought to town whatever they could sell. For centuries, the islanders had used this sled method in winter to transport their goods to the market.

To stay warm, I ran briskly beside the sled, flailing my arms in circles. The horses knew the way and followed one another in caravan style. Many of the men left their sleds, socializing with each other while the train moved on. Observing the others, I attempted to join in. I ran past Mr. Persson's sled and waited until he caught up.

"Your load of apples is really big."

"I had to bed the apples in so much hay for warmth, so I couldn't fit as many apples in as usual," he kindly answered.

Talking to Mr. Persson, my confidence rose so I waited for Mr. Renquist's sled to pass by.

"Oh, your horse is so beautiful. How old is she?"

"She's only four years old. But she's the strongest one I have for this heavy load of firewood," he replied.

The conversations up and down the train were few, dwindling as each man pulled back to focus on what lay ahead. There was plenty of time to dream and ponder on this six-hour journey. The mid-winter chill of the air seemed to vibrate against the crystal clear sky above. The stars in the dark blue sky illuminated the lonely earthlings below. The Northern Lights moved in irregular patterns with unpredictable speed and beautiful colors, intricate in their brilliance and mystique.

Just before daybreak, our train reached the ice-covered bay. Although I knew the ice had been thick enough to cross for several weeks, I prayed in my heart for a safe crossing as we left solid land behind us.

The train advanced several miles out on the endless icy desert with many more miles yet ahead before reaching midway marked by a grouping of trees which the villagers "planted". Before any winter crossings could be made, the entire "road" crossing the bay from land to land had to be marked. On an appointed day, the villagers gathered to begin the work by chopping holes in the ice every fifty feet, then plugging each hole with a five to six-foot fir tree. Without this pathway, crossings in fog or snowstorms would have been treacherous over this stretch of ice.

Our long row of horses and sleds plodded on without stopping, like a lonely row of ants lost in a no-man's land.

At daybreak, thousands of multi-faceted colors mirrored in the crystals of snow and ice, inspiring us to keep the long train moving. The faint hiss from the sled runners gently accompanied the drama of the dawn. The circle of dense firs at midway slowly disappeared beyond the horizon behind us.

One of the horses near the front violently threw up his head and snorted, upsetting many other horses in the line. Abruptly, the train halted. The man in front of me shouted, "Open seawater!"

An easterly wind had shifted the ice enough to cause a four-foot wide crevasse. From past experience, men always carried planks on a few sleds, in case of emergency. The sled master barked orders and soon a bridge over the open water was improvised. Two men on each side of the crevasse guided the speeding horses over the temporary bridge, while four others pushed the sleds from behind.

As I watched in fear, I remembered my father telling me that once a horse from our village had twisted and plunged into a crevasse. He became wedged in between the ice masses and they were unable to save him.

It was time for Flicka and me to cross. I stood up on my knees, grabbed the reins firmly, and before I realized, the horse and I had crossed to the other side. After less than half an hour, only one young horse remained. He peered into the deep hole, sucking in the vapors of the salty seawater, but wouldn't budge. The sled-master took command, ordering the horse to be unharnessed. Two leather straps were tied around his front and hind legs. The frightened animal was gently pulled down and carefully dragged across the icy boards.

Calm was restored. The sun rose, soon melting the icicles hanging from beards and hooded parkas. In the distance, Hapsal's 900-year old castle soon came into clear view, and behind it on a hill, stood the church. The shiny metal roof reflected the sunshine out to our determined train. We would reach town soon.

The last obstacle, the bank of the beach had to be scaled. Was Flicka powerful enough to pull the load up the steep hill? My apprehension was unfounded, for with both human and animal muscle, we conquered the last obstacle and the train snaked through the narrow streets of this ancient town.

Each street was lined with centuries old houses, with many of the roofs so low that their tiles could be touched from the walkway. Most of the houses were covered with heavy board siding, neatly painted in reds, yellows and blues. Curious faces peered through frost-rimmed windows reminding me that the ancient town was more than just a mass of old houses built around the castle.

Arriving at the marketplace, a cobblestone area in the shadow of the castle, we lined up our sleds according to the content of the loads. Gunnysacks filled with hay were hung from the horses' necks. I stood talking to Flicka to distract myself, trying to escape from the worry of the selling job ahead.

One prospect after another just walked by my sled, not even asking the price of my load.

"How could they just walk away?" I asked Mr. Persson, my jovial neighbor who had been my companion for so many hours.

"Don't worry boy, they'll soon be back. They are just hoping that if they act disinterested, the prices will drop down. I know they need the wood."

I tried hard to believe Mr. Persson, but my trembling hands told a different story. Two hours passed and only two loads out of seven had been sold. I couldn't go home without selling my precious firewood.

"Look," Mr. Persson whispered. "A third load has now been sold. As the number of remaining loads of firewood dwindles, you can be sure we'll hear a different story."

Those were much needed words of encouragement, but I still felt a lump in my throat. Grabbing a bag of grain, I headed towards Flicka and caught myself chewing on a handful of her oats. I gently stroked her neck.

"Don't worry, we'll sell our firewood," I spoke softly in her ear. She shook her head, not sideways, but up and down. My interpretation of her movements came quick. "You agree, I see." I relaxed and Flicka munched on her grain.

Looking over Flicka's bent neck, I spotted a man from our party tying up his horse and saw that his sled was empty. I dashed over to him.

"You sold your firewood? Where is your customer? Mr. Persson thinks we are in for a long winter. I have to convince your customer that he needs my load too."

"He was easy to deal with. Plus he gave me what I asked, five and a half *kronor*," the man answered proudly.

"Where does he live?" I asked.

After getting directions, I left immediately for his house. I spotted it a few blocks away, a whitewashed one-story building on the corner. Next to the woodshed, I saw a kind-looking stocky man in a brown knitted sweater, admiring a pile of firewood.

"Good morning, sir. Sorry to bother you, but I...I wonder if you need some more firewood? I have a load of quality dry birch," I offered.

Puffing on his pipe, he eyed me with interest. He pushed his lambskin hat back to scratch his head. It seemed as if he was trying to determine if my story was true. Slowly he stepped into his woodshed, with me at his heels.

"There's talk of a long cold winter," I said.

He studied his woodpile once again. I crossed my thumbs and two fingers behind my back, my private symbol of good luck, and waited for the man to respond.

"You come from the island far out in the sea?"

Bouncing nervously on my toes, I nodded, my head bobbing as if on hinges.

"People from the island always bring fine goods into town. And you just might be right about the long winter. All right, I'll come and take a look."

Arriving back at the marketplace, he regarded Flicka, "I once owned a beautiful horse nearly the same color, and alert like yours. She must have done well on the trip to town. How long did it take?"

"A little over six hours," I answered.

"How much do you want for your load?"

"Five and a half *kronor*," I replied.

"I'll give you six and a half if you promise to stack both your load and the other load I already bought."

"Yes, yes, I will," I heartily agreed.

I untied Flicka and grabbed the reins. "Please step on the runners behind the sled and hang on."

I was so happy to have sold my load, that I hardly remember piling the two loads for the jovial city dweller.

Six and a half *kronor*. A sum neither my hand nor my pocket had experienced before. My good news spread quickly among the traders. Flicka must have shared my feelings when she sped through the streets, her mane flying in every direction. Stepping over the threshold of the general store, I felt I had enough money to buy the entire store. Completing Mother's shopping list, I joined the men readying for the trip home. It was now almost 3 p.m., very close to sunset.

Satisfied with the long day's work, I strapped the sugar and salt that I had purchased in the sled, and nestled down just as the sled master gave his order. After everyone had been accounted for, the sled master walked to each horse and sled, quickly glancing if all was in order.

When he neared my sled, he chuckled, "I heard you did well at the marketplace. I'm sure your Father will be proud of you."

My face lit up. Undefeated by snow and ice, a heavy load and a long cold day, I thanked God and fell asleep.

It was late when Flicka pulled us up to our farmhouse. I didn't expect anyone to still be awake, but there in the candlelit window was Father. I leaped from the sled to tell him the news.

My words tumbled out even before I reached the door. "I did it Father. I sold all the wood!"

I held out the money for Father, but instead of taking it from my hand, he shoved it aside and clutched me in his arms.

"I'm so proud of you son. You left home as a boy. You returned as a man."

Angels

"Axel, come and sit down beside me," directed my brother Anders, fourteen years my senior.

His tone of voice surprised me. Why so serious I wondered? He was readying to return to mainland Estonia the next day after being home for a short vacation.

"My housekeeper is getting married and I have no time to find another one before school starts," he declared.

Anders had left our farm five years earlier to obtain his teaching certificate in Sweden. The Swedish government then sent him to Estonia to teach in one of the Swedish speaking schools, helping to preserve the Swedish language and culture abroad.

He settled in Korkis, a remote coastline village comprised of Swedes maintaining their Swedish culture and language. The villagers labored hard and long to build a new schoolhouse and proudly offered a two-room apartment within the building to Anders.

I sat down on the sofa across from my brother. He had never before talked to me as an adult. Maybe my adventure into Hapsal with the wood had shown him that I was growing up. Tufts of blond hair partly covered his light blue eyes below his high forehead. "You're thirteen now, Axel, old enough to leave home. Would you like to come and keep house for me until I find a new housekeeper, and at the same time finish your seventh grade?"

The offer was such a surprise that I couldn't answer right away. I just twisted and turned on the wooden sofa.

Finally I collected my thoughts and asked, "Can I bring my dog Lou with me?" I looked up and saw a broad smile on Anders' face.

"Yes, of course."

I wondered if he could hear the loud pounding of my heart. It sounded like a great adventure, something I couldn't resist. And to top it off, I could have Lou there by my side. "I'll pack my suitcase tonight!"

We shook hands and two weeks later my parents planted me on the ferry. Lou and I were on our way.

In the village of Korkis, life was very different from what I had experienced up to now. The Swedish dialect was interspersed with the Estonian language. Ethnic costumes were different. Often on Saturday nights, the schoolhouse was transformed to a place where people danced and sang. The Swedes had their own musical group, playing guitar, accordion and violin. Couples enjoyed waltzing, tango, and of course, folk dancing.

On the island, it was a rare occasion to eat at a neighbor's house. Here in Korkis, we were invited almost weekly for a meal with neighbors or to one of Anders' student's homes. Sampling unique dishes at their table was a treat and very different from the fare I was used to at home. Often, when dipping my spoon in a strange looking stew, I struggled to remember my manners and not ask what I was putting into my mouth.

Lou and I enjoyed socializing after school at the general store a block away. Adults gathered there to gossip and drink beer. Outside the store, Lou's tricks were in demand. She still remembered what Toivo had taught her, the portrayal of President Hoover and his wife. Lou was very popular, attending school with me and performing in the schoolyard. She patiently waited in the hallway for me until class was over.

During spring vacation, I assumed Anders and I would travel home to be with the rest of our family. My brother had other ideas though. He wanted to spend the week in Tallinn, the capital city of Estonia. I hoped we could be together, but when I was unable to persuade my brother to go home, disappointment swept over me like a dark cloud.

Lou and I walked with Anders to the train station. Would he change his mind? No. With a tip of his hat and a pat on Lou's head, Anders boarded the train. I stood on the platform and watched until even the locomotive's smoke had disappeared.

Alone back in our quarters, the first day crawled like a cat stalking a mouse. During the long night, Lou comforted me. She seemed to know when I felt chilled, for she would snuggle up close. I grew more and more restless. I tried reading. Even Lou wasn't enough. Nothing could substitute for my real wish, home. I couldn't be caged any longer in these empty rooms.

Compelled to act, an idea burst into my mind. Hadn't I sledded to the next village four miles away many times during the winter? I knew my strength. I began to develop a plan, but my success depended heavily upon the condition of the snow and ice covering the bay separating the mainland from our island.

The snow at this time of the year was two to three feet deep. During the day, the snow melted and during the night froze to a hard crust. If the crust held for several days as it often did during this time of year, I could take a short cut and reach the island in fourteen to sixteen hours, I calculated. My sled was made especially for long trips, and along with Lou, I felt confident we'd make good time.

That night, Lou and I went to bed early. She slept next to me on top of the homemade woolen blanket that Mother had sent. It was a restless sleep.

I was relieved in the morning to see that it was clear and frosty. I stepped out onto the front porch. Good, no wind. I was encouraged, ready to conquer nothing less than the North Pole. For the second time I checked the sled and its light load of food and blankets, and fastened Lou to the harness in front. I hid the house key under the stairway with a short note to Anders and set out in a southwesterly direction.

The thick crust of ice provided a continuous bridge over the deep snow. We skimmed effortlessly over endless fields, across ditches and creeks and stopped only for short breaks. We saw no one. In six hours, we had covered almost half of our trip on land.

We continued to head southwest through the late afternoon when darkness slowly set on the endless white carpet. The dark didn't worry me because the reflection of the moon in the clear sky would guide us. Far to the west, I could see the beginnings of black clouds drifting in from over the Baltic Sea. I feared the air was warming.

I stopped, concerned about Lou, for she was slowing down. I moved forward to check on the dog and her harness. As soon as I withdrew my hands from her, she dropped from exhaustion. Desperately thirsty, she began to lick the snow.

The clouds moved closer. I could feel the wind sweeping over the fields. Raindrops. Looking at the map, I figured the closest road was at least six miles away. We had no choice. We had to out-race the rain.

Resting was out of the question. I knew of several men from our island who had stopped when tired and had perished. My legs felt numb. It seemed like the soles of my feet might sink through the brittle first layer of ice. We hurried on. One hour. Two hours.

Suddenly, the long runner supporting my right foot sunk through the crust. I was submerged to my knees. Gingerly, I hauled myself up on both runners.

We moved a few feet ahead. Crack! Now both runners plunged through the crust. We were stranded. I struggled to push while Lou tried to pull the sled out of the slush. Just when I had inched the sled up on the crust and was ready to step on, it sunk back down. We were forced to give up.

Gathering my compass, one day's provision, matches and a blanket in my backpack, we abandoned the sled. My entire body was numbed, but I knew full well what would happen if I stopped moving.

Lou and I struggled on. Foot by foot. My deep-rooted instinct for survival kept me in motion. I stumbled and the cold surface of the remaining crust hit me in the face. I had fallen asleep while walking.

Now I knew. I would not make it.

I tried to crawl, but gave up. Through a daze, I saw a tree stump only a few feet away. Pulling myself up, I leaned on the stump, staring into nothingness.

Then, something in the distance. Was there a flicker of light? Or was I hallucinating?

As in a dream, I felt a presence nearby. A veiled white figure seemed to hover over us. At that moment, a renewed strength came from within me. I freed Lou from her harness, pointed at the faint light and pleaded, "Hurry."

Awareness of warmth, light and a woman's soft voice woke me. My mind told me I was still a captive of the snowy grave, but a face, and on it, a smile came into view. Her features appeared slowly, like from a puzzle, one piece at a time. I drifted in and out. Hands rubbed my limbs and poured hot tea down my throat. These caring, skilled hands brought me back to life again.

"Where is my dog?" I asked anxiously, afraid of the answer.

The woman turned and opened the door to the hall. Lou rushed to me and licked my face, but was pulled away, back into the hallway. With help from her husband, the woman helped me to a warm loft, wrapped me in thick linen sheets and heavy blankets and bedded me in hay. My head sunk deeply into the feather pillow and I closed my eyes.

How Lou had strength enough to reach the farmhouse and communicate that I desperately needed help was a mystery. Had the vision of the white figure been real?

I had no other explanation. Something had guided Lou to the house so far away. I drifted into sleep, thanking God for saving me.

It was nearly noon when I next awoke. At first, I was confused, the room was unfamiliar and it took a few minutes before I recalled the night before.

I heard a faint scratching at the door and getting up, I opened it and Lou bounded in, nearly knocking me over. The dog was followed by a woman carrying a tray laden with hot tea and pancakes.

She saw my questioning look and pulled up a chair to relate the story of the preceding night and how Lou had led them to me. I didn't remember a thing, but could sense I was well taken care of.

After my meal, the man of the house took me to my sled outside their cottage and I was thrilled that the long runners had not broken as I feared. The man urged me to rest at least another day, but seeing that the weather had cleared, I was anxious to get home to my parents.

I had no way to repay this kind couple for all their help. I could only offer my thanks. The woman packed my rucksack full with enough food for two days for both Lou and me.

Sensing my urgency to leave, they bid me farewell with the charge that if someone in need crossed my path some day, I would not hesitate to show the same care and concern as I had received.

Just in Time

Spring break at home with my family passed quickly and before I knew it, my dog and I were once again traveling on the icy roads back to Korkis, arriving safely late one night.

My brother had not yet returned from Tallin, and since he had no idea that I had also been gone, it was certain he would expect to find food in our kitchen.

Leaving Lou in the apartment, I set out on my skis to buy groceries at the larger market four miles away. It was nearly dark when I finished my shopping and packed my rucksack with supplies, carefully balancing the goods to withstand my jarring body movements during the journey home. About half way home, I stopped to adjust a loose ski binding, and looking up, was startled by what I saw.

There, in the distance stood a male figure, all alone. No skis, no snowshoes and no horse. He was a tall man, outfitted in a long dark coat and a fur cap. I shuddered; this man is in trouble. How did he get out here in this wilderness? The road was visible only in patches, mostly covered with over a foot of new fallen snow. Why doesn't he have his horse? The horse was indispensable to people out in the country and on the farm, especially during the long hard winters. As I watched the man, my thoughts went back to my early childhood and my father.

My love and admiration of horses first awakened when I was only five years old. One early May morning, my father woke me up and led me to the barn door. There, under the eyes of a loving and trusting mare, a newborn colt attempted to stand on his feet for the first time, a sight vividly carved into my memory. The mare stayed close by, following our every move. I remember when Father often led Flicka through the orchard with me on her smooth back.

During the summer, most of the islanders kept their young unbroken horses on a long strip of land projecting far out into the sea. On many Sunday afternoons, Father and I took the long walk to the pasture to see Flicka. We were very excited to see her galloping with the other horses, perhaps a hundred or more. I was amazed that my father knew almost every horse and to which farm it belonged. I didn't understand how he could tell them apart for they all looked very much alike to me.

Horses were invaluable for plowing, cultivating, transporting and logging. As a growing boy, horses were my friends, even like a member of the family. I talked to them, even confided in them.

It had started to snow again. A sharp frigid wind swirled, bringing me out of my daydreams.

The tall stranger, still in the distance, paced back and forth, trampling a deep path. He must have seen me, but I wasn't sure. I shouldered my heavy rucksack and tried to move, but couldn't. I had stood still too long. After rubbing my thighs and knees, I was finally able to move.

Now at close range, I saw that the man looked bewildered, his slack face was twisted from distress. His fur cap was askew, and a worn blanket was slung haphazardly over his shoulders. Icicles glittered in his bushy eyebrows.

The man's sled was overturned in the ditch with firewood strewn everywhere. He stood still, as if frozen to the road. Only his pained eyes moved.

Then I saw it. A horse, partially buried in the snow.

For what seemed a long time, we faced each other without uttering a word.

He finally broke the silence. "I prayed and you came, just in time." He gulped for breath and began mumbling incoherently.

I grabbed his arms and shook him. His eyes focused narrowly on me.

He blurted, "His leg is broken."

I flinched. I knew what those dreaded words meant.

A mournful cry came from the horse and the man dropped to his knees, sobbing. "I can't do it."

"What do you mean?" I choked.

He didn't answer, but turned away from me and walked to the sled. From underneath he pulled out a rifle. At first this didn't surprise me, because I knew many of the men working in the woods brought rifles along.

The man shoved the gun into my hands and without a word, he stole away towards the woods. I stared at the immense firearm. It was heavy and cold. I shrank at the fear of being too weak. I turned to tell the man I couldn't do it either. But he had disappeared.

In the accident, the horse had twisted around in a grotesque manner. He lay whimpering, a terrible mournful sound penetrating the cold air. It would be unkind to wait any longer.

I rested the gun barrel on the sled and took aim. But when I saw the terror in his eyes, my finger glided off the trigger.

The horse struggled for air, moaning in pain. There was no one else. It was up to me.

I pulled the trigger.

The shot rang out, toneless, deafening. His head fell softly into the deep snow.

In disbelief, I realized what I had done. But it was the kindest thing, the only thing. I doubled over, sank to my knees, and wretched in the icy snow. My only thought now was to escape the death-like silence. I buckled my boots to the skis, gathered up my rucksack and headed for my brother's home at the schoolhouse.

It began to snow harder. The trip home was long and my mind, heavy.

Later at home, I recounted the story to my brother, Anders. Years later my brother would say that after that day he saw a maturity in me, unnoticed before. As time passed, the impact of that deed lessened, but the look in the animal's eyes had been forever seared in my memory.

My Winged Skydiver

During my last year at junior college, I lived at a boarding house in Hapsal, Estonia, but I sorely missed the quiet farm life on our beautiful island. On weekends I often wandered to the woods nearby, taking my Bible, notebook and biology books. I loved nature and longed for the solitude I found in the deep woods.

One Saturday afternoon in late spring, I hiked through the pine woods and set up my tent just before dusk. I unpacked my meager supper, a sandwich and apples, and after devouring my meal, entered my tent and was soon asleep.

I woke up early, feeling the heat from the sun through my tent, and dozed on and off. Then suddenly, piercing cries jolted me out into the open. It sounded like birds crying in unison, but off key. A shadow glided past me, darkening the moss in front of the tent. A huge black bird landed skillfully into the top branches of a nearby giant pine.

Now fully awake, I stepped closer to the tall pine and looked up from where the cries came. There an immense nest, partially hidden came into my view. The bird, a gigantic Nordic raven was balancing on the edge of the nest feeding a half dozen hungry chicks. Their long featherless necks stretched to the edge of the nest, eagerly asking for more.

I watched the scene with great interest until my neck became tired, and then quietly returned to my tent to lie down on the green moss outside and submerge myself in memories from our farm. Around me, new life in the woods struggled to awaken.

The giant saucer shaped nest with its young inhabitants held me captive, but as the shadows stretched longer and longer, I packed up and reluctantly drifted out of the woods.

Upon arriving home at the boarding house, I went directly to my room and dropped down on my bed. The picture of the shiny black birds circling around the tall pine haunted me. I had to see them again.

That night I dreamed of ravens flying high and then low, chatting with each other and with me, in a language I thought I understood. A plan began to form in my mind. I would catch one of the young birds and train it for my companion. I didn't tell anyone of my exciting discovery. I would wait until all the details of my plan were clear.

The following Sunday, I grabbed my binoculars in hope of studying the young ravens in detail. When I saw a few feathers from the young birds sticking out over the edge of the nest, I was surprised at how much the young ones had grown in just a week.

The tree holding the nest had a smooth branch-free trunk, thirty-five feet up to the nest, I estimated. Practicing to climb up the tall pine became an important sport. Every weekend, I came a few feet closer to the very top.

One Sunday afternoon, I climbed more than half way up the tall tree and saw that the young ravens walked backwards towards the edge of the nest, relieving themselves. Their tail feathers were nearly fully developed. A couple of them were trying to walk out on the nearby branches, flapping their wings. I wondered how long it would be before they could fly. It was getting dark and time to return home, so I slid down and rested a few minutes before starting out for the boarding house. I arrived just in time to join my other classmates for afternoon tea.

"Why are you always late to Sunday afternoon tea, Axel?" grunted Leander, one of my classmates and friend.

Should I let them in on my secret?

"Wait until you hear," I answered. "I have a surprise. But first, you have to promise to help me."

Leander often took over leadership of our group of five. He responded, "It depends on what you are up to this time. Are you going to ask us to swim across the river filled with ice chunks like you did last spring?"

"No, not this time," I laughed. I studied their eager faces. In unison, the group shoved their chairs back and rushed over to me, anxious to hear. Holding up my hands for silence, I assured them that this would be a great adventure.

"I need your help to capture one of the most exquisite fliers around, the Nordic raven. I found a nest full of young ones, grown enough to test their wings. Whatever it takes, I am determined to catch one."

"Catch one? What will you do with it then?" Leander interrupted, picking pieces of bark from my clothes.

"Tame it, of course," I beamed.

"Think you can actually capture one?" Leander asked.

"I've been practicing climbing already, but I haven't yet reached the nest," I said, showing them the pitch still stuck to my hands.

Leander locked eyes with the others. "Well, what do you think? Can Axel make it to the top?"

The group shouted a resounding, "Let's find out!"

"OK, let's make our plans," I said, overwhelmed with their response. We gathered at the big table to work out the details.

The next Sunday after lunch, Leander took charge. From his room he brought out his floor length woolen coat and handed it over to Rickard. "You carry this. And Torsten, don't forget your long rope. Egil, get a good sized cardboard box from the attic."

We marched in geese formation to the woods, ready to capture one of the most mysterious aristocrats of the northern skies. Entering the woods, I took the lead, heading straight to the tall pine. We encircled the tree, and all eyes turned up toward the sky. Stunned, they stared at the nest, which was roomy enough to house any one of us, we thought.

Leander's orders came short and precise. "Each of you grab a corner of the coat and Axel, you jump up on it." With that, we tested the strength of my "safety net".

With several deep breaths and tightly clenched teeth, I leaped at the tree. My four classmates cheered as I threw my arms and legs around the slick trunk.

"Arms, legs, arms, legs," they chanted. "One, two, one, two."

I climbed until my lungs felt ready to burst. I locked my arms and thighs around the tree hoping to recuperate. Craning my neck to look down, I saw the outstretched coat appearing like a postage stamp below. Foot by foot, then inch by inch, my upward struggle slowed. Stinging salt drops from my brow blinded me. I tried to rub my face clean from the sweat against the shiny bark.

Scared. Exhausted. My last ounce of strength vanished.

Slow at first, then faster and faster, I slid down, unable to stop. Where is the coat? Can they catch me? It seemed like the green moss below rushed too fast to meet me.

Thump. I landed on the coat and rolled to the ground on my back. With my spirits crushed, but physically unharmed, I lay still on the ground, catching my breath.

Finally, Leander pulled me upright, then put his hands on my shoulders. "It's tough, but so are you. Here, eat this orange I brought and rest awhile. Try again, you'll make it."

Wiping my face with my cap, I stretched out on the large coat spread on the moss. Minute by minute, I felt the strength returning to my numbed legs and arms. The team discussed different climbing techniques. The whole group was almost as involved with the challenge as I was.

Then I looked at the pitch on my hands. I wondered if putting more on my hands, forearms and the inner surface of my thighs and knees would allow for a better grip. In minutes, we had all gathered enough pitch to cover the critical surfaces.

With a grin at my four excited classmates, I grabbed the trunk with renewed determination. Half-way up I tired and needed to rest. The pitch on my arms and legs helped me immensely in clinging to the tree without sliding down, while gathering new strength.

The four on the ground began to sing our school anthem, replacing some of the chorus with their own lyrics, "Grab, pull, grab, pull." New fire ignited in my shaky limbs.

Soon my hands locked around the first limb. I peered over the edge into the nest. Six young ravens stared at my sweaty face with beaks open, wondering what I had to offer, fish or berries. When they realized my "beak" was empty, they turned abruptly to hop back across the nest. I heard a loud whoosh. The parents were circling, coming closer and closer to the tree. One chick hesitated.

With one swift move, I imprisoned the fledgling in one hand and hurriedly tied one wing with first aid tape. With fear in his eyes, and triumph in mine, I dropped him. He gently spiraled down and landed in the coat.

The jubilant screams from my helpers were like music to my ears. Leander fetched the chick and laid him in the box. I slid down the trunk and was welcomed by hand clapping and pats on the back.

The journey back to the boarding house was filled with songs and cheers. My friends chattered excitedly as they sat down to tea. Leander prodded me to join them, but my new treasure needed all of my attention at this moment.

In the kitchen, I searched for leftovers that I might offer the hungry raven. I carried the cardboard box carefully to the attic and released him. Hopping from place to place, he picked at wood shavings. The glint of the setting sun shone through the attic window on to bright objects. Christmas ornaments, tin boxes and nails caught his eye. He inched closer and began to pick and pull at anything shiny. Seeing him fully engrossed in this activity, I left him and wandered to my room exhausted.

In two months, school would be out and I would be going home to the farm. To me, it was very natural that I would bring home the bird too. But, would Father and Mother allow it? Could I train him enough so he would obey me and not upset the farm animals? My instinct told me that "Rex", as I called him, could be trained in a couple of months to behave like any tame creature.

Every day after school, I entered the attic with a scrap of leftovers.

Rex plucked the morsel from between my fingers. Once the food was in his mouth, he would tip his head back, while I watched the food travel down his throat. He refused to drink from his water dish until I had refilled it with fresh water. Having no practice and no skill in bird training, I had to go by instinct. Over and over again, I tossed a piece of bread he especially liked towards him until he learned to catch it. Next, I taught him to catch a twig and return it to me.

Would he come to me without the bait? After repeating my plea patiently, dozens of times, finally he came to me on command. I was astonished by his intelligence.

Often he tilted his head to look at me, and then to my surprise, he flapped his wings and leaped on to my lap. I eased my hand over his head and back, gently stroking his shiny black feathers. Uneasy at first, he soon calmed down and let me tease him, by fingering his beak open and shut. We were friends. Our mutual respect and appreciation was growing.

During the next few weeks, our training sessions continued. Rex was now my constant companion, sitting on his favorite spot, a box next to my desk, partly hidden behind books. This winged creation, with one of the largest brains of all birds, was blessed with a "personality", making it possible to develop a very unique closeness in his relationship with me. When I studied at my desk, he stood close to my right elbow, watching me with great interest, and following every move of my right hand. He behaved like a participating partner, putting his foot on a loose sheet of paper or picking up something I had dropped on the floor.

Rex always presented himself as a good listener and the wiser of us two, fully understanding my teenage entanglements, helping me to solve them by just patiently listening. I am convinced that our splendid relationship was well nourished by good communication, respect for each other and an abundance of trust. Somehow, the word "pet" never entered my mind and I'm sure it never entered his mind either.

One Sunday while studying, I heard a sled arrive, then Father's voice speaking to the landlady in the hallway. When Father knocked on my door, I realized it was too late to hide the big bird.

"Hello, son, how are you?" He grabbed my shoulders. Then his eyes fell on Rex. Father stood completely still. "Oh, I see you have a roommate."

Blood rushed to my face. Stuttering, I introduced my bird. "This is Rex, a young raven. I'm training him."

"Training him? You mean, like a dog?" Father asked.

"He's very smart. Watch." I threw a pencil on the floor, and after only a moment's hesitation, Rex landed softly on the floor, picked up the pencil, and on my command, flew back up on the box.

From the corner of my eye, I could see Father's widened eyes staring. A faint smile began to form on his lips.

"When school is out, can I bring him home?" I asked.

Father ran his fingers through his well-trimmed mustache and replied, "He looks like a nice bird. But what about Mother's chickens?"

"I'll cage him if he bothers the chickens," I offered.

"Hmm, well, let's give him a try."

With relief, I thanked Father. After studying Rex from all angles, Father asked about my schoolwork then went to unload bread, butter and fruit for bartering with the landlady. After a quick lunch of soup and bread, I followed Father to the sled. We embraced and he left for home.

The four remaining weeks before the end of the school year passed agonizingly slow, but finally it was time to board the ferry for the island. Father met me at the harbor dock with the horse and buggy. Rex was encased in the box that I held tightly on my lap.

"Are you glad to be home, son?"

"Yes, I'm anxious to see Mother and I'm surprised that the grass is already lush and green. Even the buds on the trees are ready to burst. I must have missed the island more than I realized."

"Your friend in the box must be eager to get out and see where he is. Are you worried he might fly away?"

I thought about that for a moment. "No, Father, we've become such good friends. He'll never leave me."

As we drove up the driveway to our farmhouse, my thirteen-year old sister, Elsa stormed out to the wagon, long hair flying in all directions. "Oh, Axel, we've missed you so."

We sat down on the porch. "Look, Elsa. Here's a new addition to the farm."

Proudly, I lifted one corner of the box. Rex poked his head out and his black eyes darted from me to Elsa. The next moment he escaped to the tune of my sister's screams.

Calmly, he flew up to the chimney and examined every brick under his feet. When he spotted the brass buckle on the horse's halter, he landed confidently on the neck of our brown horse, cawing and cackling, but soon gave up this shaky perch. The chickens squawked and scattered in a cloud of dust as he circled over the barnyard. The sheep in the corral behind the barn panicked when he perched on the back of the big ram. Only when the frightened sheep dashed to the corner of the corral, did my winged friend return to me, alighting on my shoulder.

The busy summer work had already started: plowing, harrowing, and herding, also clearing the woods and many other chores. Rex followed me everywhere.

Rex was a very curious bird, fond of everything that was glittery. One morning, my sister Elsa was setting her combs in her hair. Rex nabbed one of them, flew up on the thatched roof of the barn and hid it. On Elsa's demand, I had to climb up to the roof and find it. Rex had buried the comb deep in the straw. From that time on, we were careful not to leave shiny objects out in the open.

Rex was my constant companion. On my bicycle tours, he sat either on the crossbar or on my shoulder, and now and then on my head, depending on the speed. When Rex selected my head, I felt insecure because his balancing maneuvers distracted me and sometimes, I would find myself swiftly off the road.

I often slept outdoors during the summer months and usually under a low-branched apple tree. Rex slept on the branch directly above my head, just an arm's length away. Sometimes in the middle of the night, Rex would drop down and stand on my chest. At first I didn't understand why, but then I would hear an animal cry, perhaps a fox or squirrel and understood that Rex had heard the sound long before I did and wanted to warn me. At sunrise, my friend Rex woke me up by pulling my blanket off with his beak, sometimes mischievously dragging it across the yard.

The first thing in the morning he demanded fresh water for his bath in a hollowed out log. He insisted I watch him while he performed his morning toilet. If I didn't comply, he just dillydallied around, postponing his bath. After smoothing out his feathers, he turned his attention to his feet, using his beak to poke and scrape, polishing and scrubbing them to perfection. Before leaving for his morning flight, he took one last look at his mirror image in the water, cocking his head back and forth, as if appraising his work. When he seemed satisfied, he soared into the sky.

One day, Mother sent me out to the woods to pick wild strawberries, and as usual, Rex accompanied me. He studied my picking technique, watching first with one eye, and then the other. After a time, he suddenly took flight. Where did he go, I wondered. I searched and found him picking strawberries several dozen of yards away. I noticed a huge pouch below his jaw, apparently filled with strawberries. Appearing restless and keeping an eye on me, he hopped away and hid. I too, in turn, hid behind a bush, hoping to discover his plans. Under a tree, he found thick green moss. Confident he was not being watched, he punched a half dozen holes in the green carpet, spacing them a few feet apart. When he left, I checked on the result of his digging pursuits. To my surprise, only one hole was filled with berries. I figured the rest of the holes were intended as a camouflage to sidetrack me.

A real adventure was to see him take flight above my head, somersaulting, rolling, then spiraling higher and higher until he disappeared. Just when I wondered if he would come back, a whistling whoosh reached my ears. Straight down he came, like a rocket. A few feet above my head he would throw out his broad wings as brakes and land perfectly on my head. Rex enjoyed the art of flying in all its dimensions, always using the air currents to his advantage.

One day late in September, Rex woke me up at sunrise, and after his morning grooming, circled around the farm and made his usual ascent into the sky. I watched him disappear as I had many times before, becoming smaller and smaller until he was totally out of sight. Anticipating his spectacular return, I waited, intensely scanning the sky.

I was totally unaware of time until Mother called me in for breakfast. Where was he?

Mother called again. I looked up, still searching. There was no sign of Rex.

Then I began to comprehend. Tears welled in my eyes.

My friend had gone. He would not return to me.

My winged friend, my skydiver, had taken his freedom to soar over mountains and perhaps even over seas, to places I could only dream about.

Rudolf Linse

I had been to the mainland to pick up a spare part for our village sawmill. On the cramped ferry crossing the bay back to Ormsö, I met Mr. Linse, a man in his fifties. By his clothing and his shoes alone, I could tell he was from mainland Sweden. He had an authoritative appearance, in contrast to me, a young man in my last year of junior college, ready to face the world.

Leaning on the aft railing watching seagulls catch fish off the stern wave, I heard approaching footsteps. When I turned, I found myself face to face with this tall stranger.

He introduced himself and asked, "Do you live on the island?"

"Yes, I do. I was born there," I answered, studying his cultivated smile that now dominated his face. I couldn't hold back my curiosity. "Are you coming to the island on your vacation?"

"No, just to visit for a day or two," he answered. "I have heard so much about this island and its people so far from mainland Sweden."

We continued to talk, looking out to sea. Mr. Linse, a civil engineer I found out, was involved in a major building project in the capital city of Estonia, Tallin. After finishing his work and before returning home to mainland Sweden, he decided to explore our island and its people. Mr. Linse was eager to know everything. His curiosity in this faraway, historically forgotten island may have come from his great interest in the Vikings. His appearance even reminded me of paintings of the Vikings that I had seen in schoolbooks. An even stronger feeling of respect took hold of me.

During the hour-long ferry trip, we fell into easy conversation. He continued to ask questions about the life and people on the island. I told him that aside from farming, fishing was the base of our economy. I explained that we fished with nets in the Baltic Sea, but with hooks in the lake. During the winter months when the shallow lake was covered with clear thin ice, my friends and I would ice-fish.

The customary long signal from the wheelhouse sounded, telling us that the ferry had now reached half way to the island.

"How many live on your island?" Mr. Linse asked.

"About two thousand, five hundred, in sixteen villages, a few villages with only two or three families. You must like to explore. Is it maybe your hobby?" I hinted.

Dropping his composure, he laughed. "Not really. I just like to see and study something different and new to me."

The old ferry bumped into the dock as usual without warning and no grace. I jumped off and scurried to catch one of the two awaiting horse and buggies, grabbing the one with rubber wheels and comfort springs, hoping to help make the five mile trip tolerable for him. After securing the better horse and buggy, I looked at him standing on the dock, taking in everything with one slow sweep. I grabbed his black leather bag and led him across the dock to the buggy.

Mr. Linse had reserved accommodations at a lodging house on the island. During the ferry ride, the thought to invite him to stay with our family had taken root. What a surprise if I brought him home.

I studied his face. He scanned the fields now carpeted with yellow buttercups and waves of blue flax caught in the summer breeze. We passed by the windmills and flowering wild cherry trees. When and how could I extend the invitation to our home?

Driving through the first village, out of the corner of my eye I saw his delight when he spotted thatched roofs on the farmhouses. "Some of the houses seem quite old, but still sturdy and very cozy in appearance. How long ago do you think these were built?" he asked.

"Many are several hundred years old. Our church, which you'll see soon, is over seven hundred years old, " I answered proudly.

Our driver didn't seem to be in a hurry. In the next village, he stopped at the water trough in the village square to let his horse drink and rest. In a way, we both felt relieved at the opportunity to walk after having been jostled around for an hour.

Was this the time I should ask him about staying with us? My heart started to thump, but just then, the driver interrupted by signaling that it was time to leave.

As we traveled again, I watched Mr. Linse's expression of surprise at almost every turn. He seemed so different, so dignified, yet so kind and interested in everything around us. He noticed every detail of the ride, even that the driver used encouraging words to the horse, instead of his whip.

Our cab wove through meadows scattered with leaf trees. A short distance from the road, a team of twelve men barely two steps apart were cutting grass with scythes. They were dressed identically in stark white shirts and black trousers. The scythes swung in perfect rhythm as the grass flew behind them, like wings of a giant bird.

"How long can they work this hard?" Mr. Linse asked.

"For four hours at a time. They start at 4 a.m. and work until 8 a.m. when their first two-hour break is taken. They start again at 10 a.m. and work until 2 p.m. and so on. Around 8 p.m., a light dinner is served and everyone goes home. After the hay has dried about a week, the women turn it over by rake to the green side for further drying. When it's dry enough, it is raked together into piles, then transported by wagon to storage sheds and attics."

As we approached Hullo, the next village at the center of the island, we moved through a stand of birch. There, abruptly before us appeared the island's Russian Orthodox Church.

"Could you stop for a moment, please?" Mr. Linse asked the driver. "Where did all these bricks come from? Was it really the Russians who built it?"

"The Russian Orthodox Church was designed by Russian architects and built with forced island labor during 1889-90. The bricks were made here on the island, but the windows and crosses came from Russia," I explained.

Mr. Linse gazed up at the five domes topped with crosses. "It looks so large here on this little speck of an island. How many can the church seat?"

"There are no seats in the church," I answered. "People were expected to stand during the service so they couldn't fall asleep."

Mr. Linse looked doubtful as I tried to explain more about the church. "It's hard to believe that Russians were on Swedish ground," he said. With a grin, he added, "When the Swedish Vikings raided Russia, I'm sure they never imagined that one day the Russians would dare to step on Swedish soil. Was the church ever used?"

"They were unable to recruit a congregation of any size," I answered, "so the Priest abandoned the island."

We were less than a mile from the *Pensionat* and it was my last chance to invite him to our home. "We'll soon be at your destination." I grabbed the railing of the cab and looked Mr. Linse in the eye. The expression on his face seemed to encourage me to speak.

My heart raced, then I heard myself stutter. "Won't you stay at our home instead?" Somewhat relieved, my next words flowed easier, "I'm sure my mother and father would welcome you as our guest. I could show you all around the island in our two wheel wagon," I rattled on.

Amused, he put his hand on my shoulder, "Yes, Axel, I would like that. I accept your invitation."

I relaxed, released my grip on the railing and proudly declared that we would have fun exploring.

We approached our Lutheran church built on a gravel bank surrounded by tall pines gently waving us welcome. I asked the driver to turn in through the wrought iron gate and stop in front of the church.

Mr. Linse stepped out, squared his shoulders and gazed a few feet above the massive oak door where iron letters were sunk into granite stone. In deep thought, he read the date inscribed on the stone, "1219".

Together, we pushed open the heavy door and stepped into the church. Mr. Linse walked erect just as the Crown Prince of Sweden had done on his visit here seven years earlier. He walked straight to the elaborately carved altar, stepped past the pulpit suspended from the wall and stopped.

Out loud he read the inscription on the wall next to the pulpit. "*Mitt Öga skall vaka Över Dig*", meaning "My eye will watch over you." And then he expressed, "I never thought to find such a jewel so far away from Sweden."

I became anxious to show him what was just around the corner. "If you follow me, Mr. Linse, there is something I want you to see. A view you have never seen before. Something which exists nowhere else in the whole world."

Stepping between tall pines and old stumps, there in front of us was the graveyard, an extraordinary sight from long ago. Huddled in groups, with some leaning slightly, and some scattered across the field, were three hundred and eighty-six sun-crosses marking the graves. Mr. Linse stood statue-still. Minutes passed by without a word. I wanted to break the silence, but when I glanced at this tall remarkable man, I held my tongue.

In a low voice he said, "I have been to many countries and seen many historical monuments, many graveyards from long ago. Many burial grounds where Vikings found their resting place. But only a dozen or two sun crosses can be found at any one location in the world, the historians have claimed."

Mr. Linse scanned the field of sun crosses again. As if stepping on holy ground, he drifted from the closest to the farthest, often kneeling and moving his hands gently over the moss covered crosses. When his hands stroked the rugged surface, I felt that it was his intent to convince his eyes of what his hands touched.

Standing next to a 36" tall cross he said, "The ancient Celtic cross, an upright cross superimposed in a circle looks very much like these crosses, except they stand on a pedestal two to three feet from the ground." His vast knowledge of ancient history, especially of the Vikings kept me spellbound.

I had almost forgotten that we were on our trip home until our driver asked if we were ready to continue our journey. I wished we could have stayed much longer in this uplifted state of mind recalling our unique history.

Mr. Linse noticed wood markers alongside the road, etched with rune-like letters, similar to what the ancient Vikings used. The letters were burned into the wood.

"What are those markings?"

I told him it indicated the identity of the farmer and which section of road he was responsible for maintaining.

Nodding his head he said, "I see they look just like the writings the ancient Vikings used on their ships and gravestones. I wonder how your island looked when the Vikings stopped over on their way to the interior of Russia down to the Caspian Sea. Many of the Vikings were traders, not just warriors and explorers. They probably stored some of their goods on your island and certainly often stayed to rest and heal their wounds," he explained.

Suddenly I realized we had left the thicket of pine and their fragrance behind us and now traveled among fields of wheat mixed with spots of wild blue carnations. The fields were fenced on all four sides to keep out the free-roaming sheep and an occasional stray animal, like a young horse or heifer. Mr. Linse was surprised to see how neat the fences were and how well they blended with the nature. I explained how the fences were made without nails. Instead they were tied together with finger-thick wild juniper branches.

He seemed to absorb every detail I described. It soon became clear to me that his perception of things depended more on his experience and imagination than what he perceived through his eyes and ears. I also wondered if traveling in the footsteps of the Vikings not only inspired him, but also made him feel at home.

As the road turned around the last bend, I saw my Mother hanging out freshly washed sheets. My heart started to race again. I knew my Father would be calm and welcoming, but I wasn't sure about my mother. She didn't like surprises of this kind, and this was a big one. Father was sawing off dry branches from the apple tree in front of our house, while my two younger sisters were stacking the dry branches on the handcart, to add to the fire burning some distance away from the house.

To my delight and somewhat surprise, my two sisters rushed up to Mr. Linse without hesitation and hugged him in unison, each trying to get a bigger piece of him. All this appeared to me like a meeting between precious friends after a long absence. They later told me they could tell right away that he was from mainland Sweden, and anyone visiting from there became an instant friend.

For a few moments he seemed lost, not knowing what to do or say, but then suddenly he bent down and hugged them, asking if they would keep the brushfire going all night. My sisters each grabbed a hand and pulled him towards the house. I tugged Mother aside and told her that I had invited him to our home as a guest.

She only said, "I have very little at home for a guest." But, graciously, Mother then stepped in front of the little crowd, welcomed Mr. Linse to our best room, while the rest of the family stood at the doorway. We all watched his face and every move he made.

I wished with all my might that he would like the bed and the room and not regret that he accepted my invitation. Right away he commented on our homemade sofa which had been built the width of a single bed with built-in bookshelves above and on both sides, forming a cozy area to sit and also sleep in. He took a book from the shelf, then touched the homemade woven blanket on top of the straw filled mattress, and announced, "This is perfect."

My second victory; he would stay.

I relaxed. Mr. Linse's response to what little we were able to offer invited me to say, "It will be a few hours before dinner is ready. Would you like to take a short walk and see if we can find any traces left from one of "*Långe Örm's* boats?" I asked.

Only a few of the islanders knew of this ship. The past generations had kept it a secret and used some of the oak hull to make tools and farm equipment, I told Mr. Linse. I wasn't sure if we could find anything left from the hull anymore, but we could just take a look. It had been several years since I had been at the site.

"Yes," he said. "I would be glad to take a relaxing walk on this beautiful island."

We stopped at the edge of the lake, now partly overgrown with sea grass, removed our shoes and stockings, folded up our trouser cuffs, and waded out to the middle. Circling around, we poked with wooden sticks into the soft bottom, in hopes of finding some remnants, but finding no signs of the ship, we gave up and returned to the shore. My grandfather was probably right when he said that most likely every bit of the ship had been removed throughout the years. Or it might have sunk too deep in the clay to find.

Disappointed, but refreshed by the vigorous exercise, we left for home.

When we arrived, supper was waiting. Newly baked bread, freshly churned butter, potatoes and smoked fish were spread on the table. Just yesterday Father had finished smoking the *strömming* (herring) in the sauna and tonight we could offer it to our guest. For dessert, Mother served wild strawberries.

"An excellent dinner. Thank you all so much," Mr. Linse said, excusing himself until morning.

The next morning I showed our guest the very heart of our farm. He wanted to see every building, all the homemade farm implements, plows, harrows, and different wagons and sleds. He had genuine interest in everything I showed him.

We walked over to a field next to our village. I showed him three windmills constructed by the villagers. Each family ground their own grains; wheat, rye, barley and oats, usually in the fall. The box-like structures were two stories high, five feet off the ground. Mr. Linse couldn't understand how two, almost three-quarter ton granite stones could have been moved from ground level to the second floor of the mill by plain and simple manpower. I didn't know either because I hadn't seen it done, but Grandfather had once explained that it was done by complex scaffolding and intricate play with pulleys, but that the bulk of the job was still accomplished by the muscles of half a dozen strong men.

Windmills in Ormsö

The entire two-story structure could be easily turned into the wind with one hand by pushing on a twenty-foot timber "handle" which was attached to the first floor of the windmill. His expression amused me, so I showed him how seemingly the whole two-story building was held together with only a few homemade bolts and nails. He admired the four twenty-foot long blades.

The next I showed him our village and sawmill. The day went by quickly and soon it was dinnertime. After we had eaten boiled potatoes and fried fish, Mr. Linse and I sat down under an apple tree heavy with new blossoms in our garden. We discussed what we had experienced in the two days traveling around on the island.

Suddenly, Mr. Linse's voice became serious. "Now Axel, tell me, are you going to settle down and become a farmer?"

His frank, business-like tone unnerved me. What would I answer? Finally I said, "Remember on the ferry over, when I told you about my tame raven that I lost the summer before?"

"Yes, I do."

"My raven finally followed his instinct. He exchanged his security for his freedom."

Mr. Linse patiently waited for a definite answer. Not a muscle in his face moved.

I looked down at my dirty bare feet, unable to hide them in the sparse grass at the bench. After many quiet moments, I said, "My raven is waiting for me somewhere out there. I want that same freedom. But I need an education first and to get that, I must leave the island and work myself through school somehow. With my Heavenly Father's help I will do just that."

It seemed like a long time before Mr. Lisne answered. "Axel, do you mean you are first going to explore the strength of your own wings and then find out what lays beyond?"

"Yes," I answered.

The next morning it was time for Mr. Linse to leave. I harnessed our youngest horse to the lightest wagon. The farewell between our family and Mr. Linse was just as intimate as the welcome, except this time there were tears.

Mr. Linse boarded the ferry and when it left the dock, I saw him lean on the railing at the exact spot where we had met. I wondered if we would ever meet again. I didn't ask for his address, nor did he ask for mine.

Spring turned quickly into summer, then fall. One day in the beginning of September, a letter from Sweden arrived addressed to *Fäll Simas Axel*, Ormsö.

It was from Mr. Rudolph Linse.

I climbed the outside ladder to the attic, a place where I often retreated when strong emotions overwhelmed me. With trembling hands, I pulled my knife from my pocket and slit open the letter.

It read, "Many greetings from your friend in Sweden, the surprised visitor to your beautiful island last summer. I hope you remember me. Many thanks to you and your parents. I had a wonderful time at your home, filled with history and beauty."

Attached to the letter was a check. I read the note in disbelief. "This is my modest first contribution to your education. There will be a check for you every month throughout this, your last year of junior college. I wish to continue helping you further in your studies until you have achieved your educational goal."

Tears, clear and sweet flowed freely down my cheeks. Endless possibilities began to form in my mind. Ever since I had performed "surgery" on my sister Katharina's new doll with a carving knife, thoughts of becoming a doctor had taken hold of me. I felt a strong desire to help people.

And now, because of Mr. Linse's faith in me, the door to that wish had begun to open. I stayed in the attic for a long time, reliving the visit by Mr. Linse and thanking God for sending him to Ormsö.

The Foxhole

Lightening struck a tree only a few hundred feet away from where I was laying.

Dazed for a moment, I didn't remember how I happened to be in this cramped foxhole. But then I recalled the night before when I had spent hours making this wartime hiding place. I was eighteen and living with my parents on the island during the summer. With Mr. Linse's funds, I had been able to attend medical school in Tartu, Estonia. At the end of my first year of studies, I spent the summer months helping on the farm. I had looked forward to being with my parents and sharing my experiences at the University of Tartu, but the quiet, sheltered life was shattered when the Russians abruptly occupied our small island.

World War II had begun. To stop the Germans from overtaking more territory to expand their power base, Russia occupied the Baltic States including our island off the west coast of Estonia in June of 1940.

The Russian forces took over Estonia's government, also our local governing body on the island. Men between the ages of 17 and 39 were being forced into the Red Army. The draftees formed an opposition group, which were called "Men of the Woods". Knowing that capture would mean the firing squad, plans were implemented to organize hiding areas in the countryside, limited to five men each. We had no guns or explosives. Our only defense was our knowledge of every inch of the island. Even so, one group of five men had been caught and shot.

A special detachment of the Red Army had been sent out to find and capture us. A few weeks earlier, nine of my classmates on the mainland of Estonia who refused the draft had been tortured and shot. Their barbed wire bound bodies were found in a gravel pit next to a main road.

The night I received my draft order, Father called Mother and me into our kitchen. Father avoided Mother's anxious eyes, and turned to face me. "Axel, you are our youngest and last son at home. Your two brothers living in Tallin probably won't be able to avoid being conscripted. But I must do everything in my power to keep you from being drafted into the Red Army."

"But soon they'll come looking for me. Mother and you will be in danger," I cried, throwing the orders on the floor.

Father explained, "There is a real fear that the Russians could harm the families of the young men who refuse the order. There are only two ways the Russians can reach our village. Our lookouts will warn us in time for Mother and me to hide safely."

Mother sat clutching a pillow as her shoulders heaved from her sobs. "Don't worry about us, son, it's you they want," she moaned. "We know many safe hiding places around the farm. Why should they hurt us? All the soldiers want is milk, bread and butter." Tears flowed over her red cheeks.

Father looked straight into my eyes, and his strong voice punctuated every word. He repeated. "I won't let them find you and take you away."

Turning to Mother he said, "It's getting late. Agneta, please pack Axel something to eat and drink, enough for the next forty-eight hours. I'll get some blankets and a shovel and Axel don't forget your knife. Find the hill I mentioned and dig a foxhole as I instructed. Try to locate it close to where the Russian patrol wagon passes. The closer you dare to observe them, the safer you'll feel in the long run."

With a "God Bless You," Father handed me the bag of sandwiches and a bottle of milk and sent me on my way, reminding me when and where we would next meet.

After a long search, miles from home, I found the hill with its ideal location overlooking the main road. The area was covered with scattered wild junipers. Anxiously, I dug out the soil from under a thick juniper, put the excavated dirt in my rucksack and transferred it to a nearby swamp. At the hole, I left a part of the roots intact, to use the juniper as a hinged lid. I planned later to make the foxhole larger and more comfortable with moss and leaves. Starting at midnight, the basic foxhole was finished just before daybreak.

A sense of accomplishment and security embraced me. Only hours ago, I had been worried and frightened, and although I was exhausted, now I felt safe. Even a trained lookout could not spot me when I raised my head from the opening, scanning like a periscope.

Sleeping through the day, and waking at dusk became my routine. The juniper lid worked well, and I often peeked out and listened. Only crickets disturbed the stillness. Now low on food and water, it was imperative that I leave the safety of the foxhole, my new home to meet up with Father.

The clear Nordic spring sky enabled me to see the hills, trees and the swamp a few hundred yards away. The narrow gravel road a few hundred feet away was clearly visible. Uncertain of what the next few days would bring, I took my bearings from the bright North star and trusted my God-given instinct that I would see or hear the enemy before they saw me. Cat-like, I leaped out of the hole, leaving the hideout and covering my tracks.

My eyes, ears and nose guided me, like a wolf being chased by a hunter. I was confident that I would be able to hear even an ant crawl up a tree. Each and every sound in the still of the night was magnified, but no human sounds, no snapping of twigs or rustling of leaves reached my ears.

Some of our villagers had said that the pungent odor from the Russian soldiers could be detected at an amazing long distance. Soap and water appeared to be strangers to them. They smoked a terrible smelling, homegrown tobacco that lingered in the underbrush long after they had passed. But tonight, the air was clean.

As I neared home, my steps slowed. In the moonlight, I saw the profusion of blossoms from the hundreds of fruit trees surrounding our little red farmhouse. Prodded on by my empty stomach, I closed in on the large birch tree and the spring just outside our orchard.

Expecting to find a note under a rock at the edge of the pond, I knelt. No note. Where is Father? My thoughts ran in all directions. Had he been captured and dragged to the Russian garrison?

Suddenly, I heard a noise. I dropped to the ground flat, expecting a bullet to whistle over my head. Pressing my body close to the ground, I tried to interpret the sound I now heard. Was it a whisper? I lay there, my heart thumping against the moisture of the ground.

Lifting my head a few inches so to hear with both ears, I heard my name. It was Father. He had been waiting in the thicket close to the large birch.

"Has everything been quiet around home?" I asked.

"No one has bothered us."

Relieved, but realizing that there was little time for small talk, I thanked Father for the supplies he brought and faded back into the woods, hurrying between trees and brush to reach the safety of my foxhole before daybreak, encouraged by Father's comforting words.

My trip back was tiring. I still experienced episodes of fright and insecurity, but also a sense of accomplishment. Finally, reaching the foot of the hill with caution, I dove into the foxhole. Once inside, I leaned against the dirt wall and prayed until I fell asleep in the safety of Mother earth.

A large beetle crawled over my face and woke me up. I saw a maze of dark red roots staring at me from the ceiling. It was late afternoon, and I had slept since dawn. It was my third afternoon in the foxhole. A pinch of sunlight filtering through green branches above collided with the red roots, making a jewel-like pattern. My bed of two blankets on a dirt mattress did not afford me a restful sleep in a semi-sitting position. The extensive root system was woven into the dirt walls surrounding me, I felt caged in a basket. But to my surprise, even as I heard the Russian wagon pass by, I felt secure and safe. My solitude became bearable as I busied myself with reading and drawing my favorite subject, horses.

A sound. Someone walked on the gravel road. I lifted the lid a bit, scanned intently, but saw nothing. I waited. Then, from behind a tree, two brown cows lumbered alongside the road, followed by a short stocky woman dressed in our island's traditional clothing, black pleated skirt and jacket. She was busily working knitting needles, pulling up woolen threads from inside a small striped bag that hung from her wrist. I smiled, thinking of the island's women who would knit almost non-stop as they walked or gathered together in groups. Relieved that it was not a Russian, I let the juniper partly fall back on the opening.

Seeing the luminous indigo sky, I predicted no rain for tonight when I was due home for new supplies. I sat down on the floor of my hideout, relying on my sense of hearing. A faint rattle from far away came closer. I waited, then spotted a wagon pulled by two tired horses, several hundred feet from the turn in the road. When the soldier-filled wagon came closer, I spied two of them sitting on a bench across the front part of the wagon frame. Quickly, I maneuvered into the most favorable position in order to study every detail. I suppressed whatever fear still imprisoned me, remembering Father's words, "Know your enemy well and your chances of survival are doubled."

The wagon came into full view, a gray mix of people, uniforms and horses. They couldn't see me even though they were only a few 100 feet away. These soldiers must be picking up supplies from the harbor and transporting what they need to the other end of the island where a group of the two hundred plus men were quartered. Or were there soldiers spread out all over the island trying to catch draft dodgers? Tonight, I hoped Father could answer my questions.

My eyes fixed intently on the soldiers on the flatbed as they passed slowly by. All twelve, probably just out of high school, seemed frozen to their seats. Their pale faces were half hidden under their oversized gray caps, and their long heavy rifles were held upright between their knees. Hunched forward, they appeared to retreat into their mammoth coats.

As I observed them closely, my lips began to form a smile. I intended to move branches out of my vision, but instead, I wiped tears from my eyes. These young soldiers, still with one foot in childhood, struggled so hard to be brave and grown-up. Maybe I sensed a kinship with them. We all were targeted to die, but the uncertainty of their fate caused me sorrow. Poorly trained, poorly armed. They seemed literally to have been sent to a foreign land to be slaughtered, to be killed by well-trained German troops who would soon conquer the island. No prisoners of war would be taken. No mercy.

After they passed, I climbed out of the foxhole. A semi darkness soon surrounded me. When I neared the meeting place, I stooped to lie down on my side when I saw Father approaching and after we greeted each other, I asked anxiously, "Have you seen any soldiers?"

"No, they haven't been in our village." Father's voice was calming and reassuring. "They've been to other villages, but not ours yet. Perhaps since we are out of the way and there are only four of you who were to report for the draft, they haven't cared to bother us yet. One draftee, as you know, lost most of his right hand in the sawmill years ago and the other has a severe birth defect on one foot. The third may have escaped to the mainland."

Father handed over three days' supplies and said, "You'd better go now. Some of them may be sneaking around. Be careful, son. God bless you and I shall see you again three nights from now."

Alone again, I walked towards the dense wood, listening and glancing back towards the farm. At the creek, I drank the refreshing water and after a short pause, hurried to my shelter under the juniper.

Shield of Hay

At midnight on my tenth day in the foxhole, I heard a faint bird-like shrill, a familiar signal. My father approached my hideout. Pushing the juniper aside, I swung up on the edge of the foxhole. Father stood with a bottle of milk and sandwiches in his hand. After a short, "How are you son?" he was quiet.

While devouring the first sandwich, I noticed Father's serious face in the light of the Nordic night.

"What's wrong?" I asked hesitantly.

With an agonizing sigh, he replied, "They caught five boys from another village hiding in the woods and shot them on the spot."

I was stunned.

"I think I've found a safer place for you. Even if your foxhole is close to their daily route, I think it's risky to stay here any longer. Especially if they bring in dogs."

When I heard Father mention dogs, my hands went numb. Father told me to get my rucksack and follow him. For an hour we hiked through dense woods, stumbling over roots and fallen trees, avoiding roads and open spaces.

At the very edge of a neighboring village, we stopped in a grove of trees to stay hidden. Across a narrow field of potato plants, we saw the outline of a farmhouse. We approached the house, and quietly stepped towards a side door that was ajar. Inside, Beret, my mother's best friend, waited. She was a small, middle-aged woman, a widow from WWI. She caught and hugged me tight.

"Have you seen any Russians?" I asked.

"Two very young Russian soldiers come every morning to get fresh milk." When she saw my fear, she laughed, "I've even made friends with them. They'll suspect nothing," she said firmly.

"Do they carry guns?" I asked.

"Yes, two old guns, weighing more than they do," Beret muttered.

Beret turned around and pulled on a thin rope above her head. Down swung a ladder from the ceiling. "You'll be safe here in the attic," she said. "You can hide in the hay."

Satisfied, Father bid me goodbye and disappeared in the darkness of the night.

Carefully, I climbed half way up the ladder to look into the space. "I'll have to move some of the hay aside so I can stretch out," I whispered. "When do the soldiers come in the morning?"

"At seven o'clock. They come to the basement door, just round the corner. Don't worry. Good night and God bless you. I'll see you in the morning after the Russians have left."

Beret woke me up the next morning by gently knocking the broom handle on the ceiling. The soldiers were gone. The aroma from the breakfast tray engulfed me. I was ravenous. I hung over the edge of the opening and grabbed the tray from Beret's hands. In seconds, I had cleaned the plate. I knew I had a busy day ahead with no time to waste.

From the entrance to the attic, I dug a channel through the hay to the other gable. I shoved the hay aside, clearing a spot big enough to stretch out and sleep. Light filtered between the spaces of the wallboards at the other gable, enough to read by and to view the outside. In an emergency, a few boards could be pushed out for an escape route.

Finishing, I compressed an armful of hay and tightly bound it with wire so I could plug the entrance to the channel from the inside. I had made my shield of hay with an invisible entrance. At sundown, I fell asleep, confident that I had done my best to hide myself. The rest I would leave up to God.

Early the next morning while busily picking straw from my hair and clothing, I recalled what Beret had said about the two soldiers. I wanted to see them for myself. It was not a lack of trust toward my mother's friend, but just thinking about their guns unnerved me.

Between cracks in the gable, I could see the gate barely a hundred feet away. It was nearing 7 a.m. I glanced at the gate and then down at my trembling hands. I willed my thoughts back to the encouraging moments when I arrived at this house. But the behavior of my hands didn't stop. Suddenly I heard a noise outside.

A brown and white heifer stood at the gate rubbing against the post. Now it was several minutes past seven. Maybe the soldiers are not punctual after all.

Just then, I heard them laughing. They were partly hidden by the gate and the heifer. What I saw were two poorly dressed soldiers with guns weighing heavily down on their shoulders. One scratched the heifer between her ears and the other gently stroked her back. At the sight, the tension in my body ebbed away. They were not fierce killers. They were farm boys, just like me.

The hems of their long coats dragged on the ground, and their pale faces were nearly hidden under the caps sliding off their heads. Two teenagers having fun wearing their father's clothing, I thought. They had placed their rifles against the gatepost while attempting to stop the heifer from following them into the yard. Through the cracks I saw the animal swiftly shoot through the gate, pursued by the two gun-less soldiers stumbling over their large boots and coats. I suppressed my laughter. Beret suddenly entered the scene with a long stick and cussing under her breath, rounded up the heifer. With united effort, the errant animal was soon back in her pasture.

I couldn't help it, I felt a strong empathy for the two young men. My thoughts drifted to their homes and their parents, remembering what Beret had said yesterday. The Germans were taking no prisoners and showed no mercy towards the Russians. And as things now stood, the Germans could reach our island in a short time. They would bury all the Russians in a matter of hours, including these two.

The boys I viewed every morning came from a faraway place, where their families probably had lived for centuries, always struggling to survive under a government who treated its citizens as expendable items. Knowing they had orders from their superiors to shoot me on sight, I felt like a disposable item too, but seeing how young they were and how innocent they seemed, that feeling vanished.

Watching the two Russians became a part of my morning routine. Each day, my study of the two began when I spotted them arriving from a couple of hundred feet away. I focused on their walk and their body posture and many other details. As they came closer to the gate, I scanned their faces and their expressions. I tried to look for any bloodstains on their hands or clothes. Each day, I feared that they might have been replaced by tougher soldiers, but when I saw their familiar faces, I felt comfort in the two and their routine.

If every detail looked the same as the previous day, I relaxed. There were still times when I felt numb, thinking of the future and what would happen and when. There were times when watching a spider weaving a web above my head helped me escape my tortured mind. Even an ant crawling over the straw with her burden held me spellbound for hours, pulling me a few inches away from my tension. Only a few times during these long months did I feel close to panic, as if a flame was consuming me from the inside out. When I didn't move for a long time during the day, Beret always checked on me, bringing an encouraging word or news from Father.

Six weeks in the hay passed. The two uniformed daily visitors almost seemed like part of the family. One Sunday morning while reading my Bible, I lost track of time. When I glanced at my watch it was half past seven a.m.

I peeked through the cracks. There was no one in view. I became worried, but before crawling through the channel to ask Beret if there was any news, I took one last look through the cracks. There they were, quite far away, across the field. Something moved between them. As they came closer, this something took shape. A huge German shepherd. I could outrun the Russian soldiers with their constrictive clothing and heavy old guns, but a German shepherd would tear me apart in minutes.

Had something made them suspicious? Could I escape from the attic and reach the nearby woods while they were at the other gable?

I heard Beret's loud and cheerful greeting to the dog, seemingly ignoring the soldiers. Don't move, I hammered into my head. Every limb tensed for escape, but my mind said no. After long moments, I thought I heard the gate open, then close. Still I didn't dare to look.

Beret signaled on the ceiling. Three knocks, pause, two knocks. As I snaked through the channel towards the lid, I felt every beat of my heart.

Beret's dark brown hair, then her small face appeared through the opening in the ceiling. My eyes caught her smile and the words, "A pup, just a pet, a lovely dog. The soldiers probably miss their pets at home. I don't know enough Russian to find out where they got the dog. It's not from our village though."

I sighed deeply. My feeling of security gradually returned and I crawled back into the safety of my hideout and continued to read my Bible.

Another month slowly glided by. Out in the field, the potatoes had already dropped their blue flowers. The wheat and rye had been harvested and threshed. The cherries and early apples from our orchard had been picked and sold in town.

My worry about Mother and Father's safety had eased. Beret informed me that in the beginning, they had been questioned frequently about my whereabouts, but my parents' story must have been convincing, for they had not been further harassed.

Surrounded by walls of hay, imprisoned, in fact, I felt totally controlled by my circumstances. During the Russian occupation of the island in 1940-1941, the soldiers had gone from farm to farm to confiscate the battery-powered radios. In spite of the severe penalty risk, a few families had secretly kept theirs hidden. Thus, the news of the war had been kept current on the island.

In the very beginning of September, we knew the Germans were preparing to invade the island. On the ninth of September at 3:45 a.m., the eruption of heavy gunfire woke me. In a few moments, my brain went into full gear. In my mind, I tried to liberate myself from the fetters that had paralyzed me for so long. One moment my body felt like jelly, the next moment, it felt like a steel spring.

Leaving the shield of hay during the battle could be suicide. Beret had learned from two veterans from WWI still living in her village, that we would see a tough battle when the Germans landed on the coasts of Ormsö. There were 500 plus Russians facing 150 Germans. The Russians had a few attack airplanes on mainland Estonia, but the Germans didn't seem to care, declining to counter attack by their *Luftwaffe*. It was clear that the fighting had to be short and fierce if the Germans were to win.

I was determined not to abandon my fragile shelter. Apparently sensing my distress, Beret lifted the lid at noon that day and whispered, "The Germans are advancing fast."

"Are they close to our village? Is the Russian unit still here?"

"I don't know. Everything in our village is quiet."

She closed the lid and I was alone with my thoughts and my fears.

One moment I felt ready to fight. The next moment, I felt incapable to even move, straining to breathe. This war on the island could last for many days, maybe weeks. To stay put was to survive.

In the distance I heard more canons and gunfire as the thundering battle neared. The intensity of the battle raged even into sundown on the first day.

I wondered if at this very moment my two teenaged soldiers were engaged in fighting. Their pure absence seemed to turn my life upside down. I missed watching them pick weeds from the potato field and with delight, feed the heifer on the other side of the fence. It seemed the heifer was their only true and dependable comrade. Would these two boys survive the battle and go home?

During the long afternoon, I felt anesthetized by the noise. I peeked through the cracks in the gable and saw a wonderful sunset. Light clouds moved by a gentle breeze, wove the remaining sunlight into a gold, blue and red tapestry, reminding me that God was still in charge.

The next morning at sunrise, the eastern sky put on a brilliant show and appeared with a more distinct red, blood red, I thought to myself. After a while, the heifer ambled to the gate searching for her friends, and finding none, she wandered into the woods.

I tried hard to distract my mind from the explosions and gunfire, now increasing in intensity, spreading across the island. It sounded like the inferno surrounded the village, but Beret assured me that the battles had not touched the village yet. My thoughts wandered to the daily simple routine on our farm, *Salt-Simas Gården*. But more than anything else, I agonized over the interruption of my studies at the University. Would I be able to return?

On the afternoon of September 13, 1941, the explosions and gunfire suddenly ceased.

My yearning for home was overwhelming. I pulled up the lid to the room below and dropped the ladder. Just when I stepped on the first rung, Beret appeared, holding up her hands and ordered, "No."

"Isn't it all over?" I wailed. "I don't hear any more shooting."

"You must wait for your father. He'll decide when it is safe to leave here," was her short response.

Disappointed, I crawled back to my gable. I flattened my face to the boards with one eye focused intently through the widest crack. I waited. Just after two hours had passed, I spotted Father. He was crossing the potato field with the broadest smile I had ever seen on his face.

I scrambled through the hay, down the ladder and out the door to meet his open arms. We had no words, only tears.

We ran all the way. At home everything looked so different, as though I had somehow acquired new eyes. I raced back and forth from the stable to the orchard, from the house to the pasture, taking in every detail, all that I had missed during my time away.

Had my two young Russians survived? I must know. Father told me where the battle of the island had ended, at the lighthouse in Saxby. I knew I would find the answer there.

Sweat dripped down my face as I ran the narrow dirt road through the woods towards Saxby, some four miles away. Nearing the lighthouse, I saw a score of German soldiers washing blood from the entrance of the lighthouse with buckets of water and brooms.

A tank with bulldozer blade was shoving dirt into a ditch. I peered into the cavernous hollow. A mass of tangled bodies, bloody uniforms and boots lay silent, slowly disappearing under the black earth.

In my hideout, I had vowed that if my Russian friends did not survive, I would somehow retrieve their dog tags and send the tags home. I had wanted to tell their parents how much their sons had meant to me during all the months I had been in hiding from them. Hiding in an attic and watching them through an inch crack in the gable. In reality they were my enemies, but I could see they were just boys, innocent of the deadly assignment, who might rather handle shovels than guns. As the ditch filled with dirt, I realized that my desire was impossible.

The Russians had been defeated and Estonia was free. It was time to resume my studies at the University and I began making plans to leave the island for Tartu.

Graz

After the Russians had been routed from our island, I wanted to return to the University of Tartu in Estonia and continue my medical studies. The monthly check I had been receiving from Mr. Linse was cut off, probably due to the political upheaval caused by the confusion of the Russian leadership. It was a terrible blow. What could I do? I would soon run out of funds.

My oldest brother, Anders, a schoolteacher, had been deported to Russia. His wife begged me to come to Korkis and replace him at the school. There was no time to grieve over his absence. I packed my belongings, hoping to return to Tartu next fall.

At the end of the year after finishing teaching, I searched for a way to continue my studies at the University, but failed. In desperation, I turned to my brother-in-law, Sven Rydén, an officer in the Swedish Army.

At the time, Sven, a Lt. Colonel had volunteered in the Finnish Armed Forces during the Finnish-Russian war. During that war, Finland had allied itself with Germany and when the Russians had been conquered, some of the officers who had volunteered to fight with the Finns were asked to join Germany's Armed Forces. Sven accepted the invitation.

The German high command considered the Finns, Swedes and other Scandinavians as dependable, trustworthy and brave soldiers and often recruited them ahead of other nations. Sven received a job at Berlin headquarters.

On leave, Sven traveled to Ormsö to see his wife Maria, my sister, who was running an eight bed hospital-like facility on our island. I was visiting my parents at the time. In my desperation, I told Sven of my dilemma. He made some calls to Berlin and Graz, Austria and after a few days he informed me that he had been able to obtain a scholarship for me at the University of Graz. The papers and a railroad ticket arrived a week later.

I now stood at the railway station in Tallinn, waiting to board a train for my journey to Graz. The old locomotive was engulfed in steam and smoke as the conductor whistled the signal for departure. In the passenger cars, there were no empty seats, but I found a corner where I placed my rucksack on the floor and sat down.

Some hours later, I stepped out on the platform to exercise and get some fresh air. In nearly all the villages we passed through it seemed like I saw only women and children, with sadness and hardship showing on their faces. Returning to my corner, I slumped down on my rucksack and fell asleep wondering why there were so few men in these villages.

A sharp whistle woke me from a deep sleep and looking at my watch, I realized we had been traveling for many hours. The train stopped and I stepped off to exercise my legs. I was surprised that we had already reached Konigsberg.

A wonderful aroma reached my nostrils from a kiosk next to the station. Behind the counter, a man in a white apron vigorously stirred soup in a large pot. I pulled a few coins from my pocket and bought a bowl of steaming potato soup and while enjoying the homemade taste, I noticed a billboard advertising a movie starring the famous Swedish actress, Zarah Leander.

Everything was forgotten, the trip, the train, my plans. On the spot, I chose to stay over and see the movie. The next showing was several hours away, so I decided to take a walk and familiarize myself with the first German town I had ever seen. I spotted a park nearby surrounded by a hedge. Stepping through an opening, I stood face to face with a column of men marching, four abreast and ten in length, guarded front and rear by German soldiers with guns.

The procession confused me. The striped clothing looked so strange. Their faces were downcast. An offensive smell of fermented sweat hit my nostrils. Something tore into me, something very sad and painful. As the column dragged past me, I followed them with my eyes. Something didn't fit. They weren't convicts or soldiers.

And most disturbing, why had a large letter "J" been sewn on every shirt back?

I became aware of an elderly gentleman slumped at the end of a bench, digging in the gravel with his walking stick.

"A rucksack?" he asked without turning towards me. "Are you traveling?"

"Yes, I'm going south, to Graz, to continue my medical studies," I replied.

I waited for him to respond, but he made no sound. He seemed reluctant to talk. His eyes were firmly set on the soldiers and their captives marching slowly across the field.

"Who are they?" I asked.

He spoke almost as if he feared being overheard. "You don't know? You must be from far away, perhaps from the North?" He wouldn't look me in the eye. I felt uneasy as the minutes passed.

"Yes, I'm from a small island off the coast of Estonia. This is the first time I've been this far from home and everything is so different from what I expected."

His shoulders tensed as he turned to face me.

I repeated my question. "Who are those men? And why are they being guarded?"

"They're Jews," he replied.

The old gentlemen raised from the bench as if burdened by a heavy load and slowly shuffled away. The field was now empty. The young men in the striped clothes were gone.

I wondered what it all meant. Had I made a mistake in coming here? My optimistic view of the future suddenly seemed empty, like a room without windows, but I knew I had no choice but to continue south to my destination.

In the morning, I caught the next train. As I studied my map, it was apparent that the train was on a detour, so I asked the conductor about it. His answer shocked me. The train that I had abandoned yesterday had been bombed!

The remainder of the trip to Graz was filled with frequent stops and many hesitations, but we finally arrived at noon two days later.

Stepping off the train, I felt as if I was not only in a different country, but in a different world. Walking away from the station towards a mountain, I was struck by the quietness and the beauty of the centuries old gothic cathedral in front of me. I wondered if this city surrounded by mountains had been sheltered from the war.

It was time to find my way to the University. Falling back on the German I had learned at school, I asked for directions and soon found myself at the foot of Schlossgebirge, a low mountain peak. A rider in military uniform astride a spirited horse approached me from the opposite direction. Stopping in front of me he inquired if I was lost.

"I'm looking for the University," I replied.

The horse pranced in place until he commanded, "Follow me. I just came from there."

Up ahead I saw the complex of brick buildings. The officer stopped and asked politely with just a shadow of a grin, "Are you one of the new medical students?"

"Yes, I am," I answered.

He rode up to the gatepost and rang the bell with his short whip. A guard appeared from inside the complex, opened the narrow side door and asked for my papers. The horseman tipped his whip to his cap in salute and rode off.

The guard handed me over to another man who led me to a room on the second floor.

"Put your things down and follow me." He took me down the hall to a larger room and once inside, he clipped, "What size do you wear?"

His question caught me off guard. I looked around the room and was bewildered by what I saw. Hanging on long metal racks were German army uniforms. Next to these stood tall shelves with cubbyholes filled with socks, shirts and boots. I was baffled.

"Am I to wear an army uniform?" I asked.

He barked his reply, "My orders are to outfit you."

"But what is this all for? I'm supposed to study medicine here."

"You'll be informed further in the morning."

With that, he pulled a set of clothing off the rack, handed the items to me and motioned towards the door.

"Breakfast is at 7 a.m. Wear your uniform."

There was nothing else to do but return to my room.

My quarters were sparsely furnished with only a bed, table and chair. I hung the uniform on a hook behind the door and sat down. What was this all about? What did wearing an army uniform have to do with medical school? A very uneasy feeling began to take hold of me. Things were not as I expected. Hopefully, in the morning I would know more.

At 6:30 a.m. I was awakened by the bugle call. I hurried into my clothes, hoping to reach the dining hall early. Entering the cavernous room, I saw a U-shaped table in the center and at the head table sat four men who appeared to be in charge. The man in the center looked up and motioned for me to come forward.

"Welcome to the University of Graz," he spoke. My eyes moved to his shoulder pads where a grouping of stars were pinned. I recognized his rank, a Colonel.

I answered him according to protocol, then took my seat. There were twenty other students sitting down at the table. They greeted me and we exchanged small talk, but I was anxious to finish so I could meet the Dean of the University. Surely he would be able to answer my many questions.

After a breakfast of warm porridge and dark bread, I made my way to the Dean's office, knocked on the door and heard, "Enter." Two men sat at the desk, both in military uniform. I laid my papers on the table.

The older man quickly viewed my documents, then began, "This University is now in the hands of the German army."

"I don't understand. When I accepted this scholarship, I was told nothing of this."

His eyes showed sympathy, yet his tone was firm.

"You are to function as a field medic for week-end assignments. This will not interfere with your studies." He stood. "You are dismissed."

I had been in the room less than five minutes, but in that short time, realized I had made a grave mistake in coming here. What I had seen since leaving home began to close in on me. As I had done back home when distraught, seeking solace outdoors among the trees, I now found the same strength sitting under an old pine in a park close to the University.

Two days later I was given papers ordering me to report to a boot camp in Sennheim, at the border between France and Germany. Thousands of volunteers were being sent there from all over Europe. The next six weeks were filled with strenuous activities where we were pushed to our emotional and physical limits. Finally, after six weeks, my time at Sennheim was finished and I returned to Graz in the early fall of 1943.

I poured all my energy into my studies. The autopsy table at the University became the focus of my fall semester. The anatomy, pathology and the diagnostics involved were comprehensive. A sharp scalpel and a steady hand were paramount. At night, the only light in my room came from a single bulb from the high ceiling. I could barely see the print in my textbook, but how to remedy the situation? After some thought, I placed my chair on the table, climbed up, taking with me a smaller table, and spent my evenings perched close to the ceiling.

Working two to three days weekly as a medic with troop transports which were criss-crossing Europe enabled me to forget the grueling monotony of dissecting and studying.

With almost regular intervals I passed through Berlin where Sven, my brother-in-law, and I met in a restaurant not far from the Central Station. He was always curious about my travels and would ask many questions. I didn't think much about it until early in December, when we met after I had returned from a troop transport to Eastern Europe.

Sven moved closer. Would he ask me again about the details of my trip? A look of pain crossed his face when he whispered, "Whatever I have asked you and what we have spoken of is between you and me, and you and me only."

I suddenly realized that something had happened since we last met. Had Sven become a secret agent for the Allies in Europe? And I, unwittingly, a co-agent? Would my close connection with Sven jeopardize my plans to leave Graz? I wanted to scream, to demand that Sven tell me more, much more. But he remained silent.

Slowly, we left the warmth of the restaurant. At the moment we said goodbye, Sven grabbed my hands tight in his iron grip as if he was drowning.

Christmas of 1943 was approaching. I wanted to see Sven again, but no one knew where he was. Then I recalled a Capt. Jouko Itälä, a volunteer from Finland whom I had met at Sennheim and who was also working with troop transports. He might know something about Sven I hoped. I arranged to meet him a few days later at a coffee shop.

After talking for a few minutes about his work and my studies and the east front, I carefully guided our conversation towards Finland, Sweden and Sven. I delayed directly asking about Sven's whereabouts, afraid of the answer. I knew that this Captain had been friends with Sven for some time.

Leaning forward I said, "I'm concerned about Sven, my brother-in-law. I haven't heard from him for almost three weeks. We used to meet often, sometimes every week. Suddenly, I can't find him." I studied his face.

Slowly, Capt. Itälä refilled his cup of tea, pulled out a cigarette, but made no move to light it.

I looked into his eyes. At that moment, I knew the reason for his reluctance.

"I'm sorry," he said, "Your brother-in-law, Lt. Col. Sven Rydén is dead."

"How?" I stammered. "What happened?"

"He was shot, trying to escape. It happened on a dock in Denmark."

"Who told you?" I asked.

"A friend was waiting for a troop ship from Norway and witnessed the shooting."

I was stunned. I couldn't comprehend the scope of it. But I realized the danger had escalated and I might also end up dead.

When the opportunity came, I must find my way back to my family in Sweden. It was now obvious to me that the Germans were allowing me to study so that when I graduated, they would essentially "own" me.

At night I struggled with ideas and plans.

Many students were requesting Christmas vacations. Would I be allowed to travel? One morning after breakfast I decided to make my request, and entered the Dean's office.

"Yes?" said the Dean, without looking up.

I took a deep breath. I knew this was my only chance to leave. I had rehearsed my speech during the last few days, hoping not to reveal my real reason for the request.

"A few of my colleagues have been granted a leave over the Christmas break. I am here to request the same." Having spoken, I relaxed a bit and waited for his reply.

"Do you want to go home?"

"Yes, sir. My family is now in Sweden. May I travel there?"

The Dean swiveled his chair away from me and received a well-worn manual from his assistant. I stood rigid as long minutes passed while the Dean turned the pages one by one.

Finally, finding the page he sought, his bony finger ran down a list, stopping at a line.

With that, he turned to face me. "No, not to Sweden."

Blood rushed to my face and I blurted, "Perhaps Estonia?"

Taking a second look at the list, he smiled and replied, "Yes, I'll sign your papers. They'll be ready in the morning."

I thanked him and left.

Early the next morning I packed my rucksack with only the bare necessities, picked up my papers and walked out the door.

I was tempted to look back, to preserve in my mind the University buildings, but when the word freedom loomed in my thoughts, the school and my studies here didn't matter. Could I get away before my real plans were discovered?

I ran to the train station, arriving just in time to board the train leaving for northern Europe.

From Estonia, I would make my way to Ormsö, and from there make an attempt to reach Sweden.

Escape

It had taken me nearly three days to make my way from Graz back to Ormsö.

Fearing another onslaught of Russian military caused the islanders to begin to leave for mainland Sweden. During 1942-1943, the Swedish government intensified their efforts to evacuate Ormsö. Local German authorities restricted the immigration in the beginning: the very old and the sick were among the first allowed to leave during the latter part of 1942. With the help of my older sister who now lived in Sweden, my own parents were allowed to leave soon after midsummer of 1942.

It was now 1:30 a.m. In the woods, around me crouched eleven young men. A grove of tall junipers close to the snow-covered beach barely hid us. The Nordic sky was clear. The reflection from the glimmering snow revealed our faces, some with a spark of anticipation and hope, others with fear. What would become of this band of young men thrown together in time of war?

My hands trembled. The chill in the pit of my stomach tortured me.

When I had arrived back home from Graz, I found my village was nearly deserted. When my father, along with other islanders realized that our young men would be drafted into the German army, the idea of building escape boats took shape. During the last several months, many of the young men had escaped to Sweden via Finland. The few young men remaining in the early spring of 1943 were in hiding, hoping that another small boat would soon be ready to cross the gulf to Finland. The escape was risky and many boats had been lost.

Upon arriving home, I found that our neighbor, Gertrude, was one of the few remaining in our village. She informed me that a 23' escape boat was being built in the woods, a boat my father had invested time and material in before leaving for mainland Sweden. The long summer days were perfect for boat building, a mission that became urgent as time passed. The tedious farm work had been dropped by most of the men; instead they were consumed with an urgency to finish as many boats as time allowed. All the materials for the boat were transported in secret to a secure place, well hidden and far away from the traveled roads. The hammering and sawing was muffled somewhat by the thick woods, yet look-outs were placed in critical areas.

The keel of the boat, being the heaviest portion, was crafted from a tree felled on the spot. The boards, nails and ribs were brought to the site, bit by bit, each man or father supplied a part of the necessary materials. One neighbor had an old motor hidden in his barn, other islanders hid oars, oil and fuel, all in preparation for the departure.

Repeatedly, Gertrude, a woman in her fifties, would walk the four miles to visit the Trustee in the next village. My father had asked the Trustee, Thomas, to supervise our departure. Thomas knew all the details important for an escape, from the weather predictions to the installation of the motor and finally, choosing the departure date.

I was grateful to Gertrude for caring for our horse since my parents had left. Her teenagers had already escaped to Sweden and her husband had died recently. She was glad to be involved while she awaited the next ship to Sweden.

Finally, late one night Gertrude received the news that the boat was finished and ready to leave. She raced home to notify me. Without delay, she harnessed our horse while I gathered my things into my rucksack.

We silently sneaked through the woods to the hidden boat, stopping frequently to listen for German patrols. Would this be the last time I would see my beautiful island, these familiar trees and sandy beaches, my childhood playground?

At the boat, we boys waited impatiently for Thomas. Quietly, the twelve of us quickly set to work, hooking up the lines to the horse to pull the boat to the beach. Look-outs had assured us there were no Germans in the vicinity, but still we were wary. The horse struggled valiantly to pull the heavy boat, and we helped, pushing from behind. We stopped half a mile from the water's edge at a spot camouflaged by tall junipers. Our last thrust lay ahead, across the ice-covered beach and into the sea.

We knew Thomas would come, but when? We counted on his experience with boats and seas, but more than that, our hope-starved minds needed some words of encouragement.

As I stood leaning on the boat with one shoulder, one of the younger boys seemed to take comfort leaning on my other shoulder, plucking nervously at my sleeve.

Just then I heard something.

"What's that?" I whispered, hearing the crunching of snow only a few feet away.

We dropped to the ground.

Suddenly, a tall man eased silently into our midst. It was Thomas, dressed in a dark heavy coat, with a fur hat pulled far down. All twelve of us stood up at attention.

"Did you get my message?" He asked in a low, but authoritative voice.

We nodded in unison. "Yes, sir, we all have our survival kits," we answered, hoisting our bags into the boat.

"I must check on the ice down at the beach." With the ice pick on his shoulder like a soldier with his gun, he stepped out of our ring of renewed hope. His tall body vanished into the white emptiness. Only the refreshing smell from the junipers penetrated the cold air.

"Let's try to move the boat a few feet before Thomas returns," I suggested.

We pushed. We pulled. Nothing happened. I walked around the boat, noticing that in front the snowdrift was too high. Martin, the young man who had brought the motor, instructed everyone to trample down the snow. We were thankful for this diversion from the tension. We pulled again. Not an inch.

"We'll wait for Thomas," someone whispered.

Time ticked away. Suddenly, we heard a faint rustle from behind. Unexpectedly, four girls appeared out of the woods. Their faces were nearly covered by dark shawls, only their eyes were visible.

One by one, without a word, they crawled over the railing at the midsection and into the boat. We were stunned. Three days of food and water and some fuel. And twelve of us boys. The boat was already loaded to its limit. Didn't they understand this boat had been built to save the young men from being captured and forced into the German Army?

My anger surfaced, yet I felt empathy.

The young men, pale from fear, drew closer to each other. I looked from face to face. Their eyes pleaded and their lips whispered, "stop the intruders". I couldn't. My feet felt as if shackled to the trampled and frozen ground.

Just then Thomas returned. He stopped at the boat where the frightened young girls huddled. He shook his head in pity, stretched out his hand and calmly said, "Come. The Germans haven't hurt anyone on the island. The next Swedish ship will soon come to pick you up." He picked a few icicles from his mustache. "These young men are going on a dangerous trip."

Regret was written on the girls' faces, yet smiles emerged in an attempt to make amends. Quietly, the four girls climbed out and disappeared back into the woods.

I asked Thomas the Trustee, "Are you going with us?"

"No, when you're safely in the water, I have done my job. There are more young men on the island who need my attention." Then he turned to Martin and said, "I'm putting you in charge. Do you have enough gasoline?"

Martin shook his head, "No, but hopefully we can reach close to the Finnish coast before we run out. If not, we have our oars."

"You know everyone on the island is praying for you. You'll make it."

I watched Thomas slowly disappear back into the woods.

In the stillness of the cold air, I thought I heard him sob.

The Life Line

It was past midnight. We twelve young men stood anxiously around the 23' boat. Each of us placed one hand on the railing and waited for the signal to shove off.

Foot deep snowdrifts separated us from the icy water of the Baltic Sea.

We knew that after this morning we might never see our island, our homeland again.

The chill of the night and the shivering fear of being caught and shot by the Germans made it difficult to concentrate on the task ahead. Our fear increased further when we realized that there was no chance to test the seaworthiness of the newly built boat.

Our eyes were focused on Martin, the young man who had brought and installed the one cylinder motor. Martin, at twenty-two, five years older than most of us, assumed the leadership. He stepped into the midst of us, adjusted his gray fur cap and gave orders.

"Keep your eyes on my white handkerchief. I'll stand close to the stern and give the signals."

Silence took over. No whispers. No questions. In the spare light, one could still see all the faces, now turned towards the stern.

The white flag shot up. Martin held it high above his head. We waited.

Just then, Martin jerked his head to the right. We all heard something, carefully placed footsteps. Germans? Had we been caught even before we left the shore?

Out of the shadows appeared a stooped form, carefully inching towards where Martin and I stood at the stern. He stopped two feet away from us. Relieved, I recognized him. He was the grandfather of the two boys I had hidden under the floor of our stable. Their schoolteacher parents had been captured by the Russians when all educated people and their families were deported. The two boys were visiting us at the time and were spared.

The grandfather held up a container. "I heard you are short of fuel. Take this," he insisted, and pushed a ten liter canister into my hands.

We were overjoyed. Without another word, he disappeared in the darkness.

All eyes fixed again on Martin's white handkerchief.

The white flag plummeted. Martin and I pressed our shoulders to the stern while the others grabbed the railing, and together we pushed the boat to within a few dozen feet of the open water.

Many of us were consumed with thoughts about those who never made it across. Martin walked calmly to the very edge of the ice, carefully tapping his foot to test the strength of the ice. Could the ice break too soon and too unevenly, capsizing the boat before we managed to get it afloat?

Martin asked, "Look, do you all see that large gray rock sticking through the ice?"

We nodded.

"The boat will not be afloat until we are beyond that rock. At that moment, be ready to jump into the boat." Without further delay, he ordered, "Grab, ready, go."

When we reached the rock Martin shouted, "Everybody in the boat. Wrap the oarlocks with sheepskin you'll find in the forward locker and man the oars." He quietly added, "We have more than sixty miles to cover. Row with all your might and let us all pray, each to himself. The next four of you will take over in half an hour. We have to be out of sight before dawn. I'll start the motor when it's safe. Let's all hope and pray there will be no Germans, no Russian ships or U-boats."

In spite of our "captain's" concern about the dangers, he spread optimism by his authority and knowledge. The rhythm of the oars dipping gently into the smooth water was calming, bringing hope to our minds so full of turmoil.

The rest of us sat like human shadows, petrified, shivering and trembling, as we glided farther and further from land. Martin stood in the center of the boat, combing the waters and shore with his wakeful eyes. Soon, the fog would dissipate and we would be able to navigate by the stars, and at the same time, I could check on my old compass.

With regular intervals, Martin checked on the bilge. "Only a few inches of water, as yet," he mumbled to himself. "We can handle that. Our freeboard is over a foot. It's enough, if the seas stay calm."

The four oarsmen were relieved and the boat continued to inch ahead. Cramped, we huddled close to keep each other warm. A strong feeling of togetherness drifted into our thoughts, fueled by the realization that if we reached Finland, we'd reach it together. If we perished, we'd perish together.

We were still under the cover of dusk when I saw Martin prepare to start the old motor. Suddenly, he signaled the oars off the locks. A deafening noise exploded. When I felt the boat speed ahead, I saw grins all around.

Just before dawn, Martin looked into the dark sky at the navigational stars. I could tell he was figuring out the deviation of my old compass.

Sitting close to him at the stern, I asked, "Does my compass work?" I knew we were going to need it during daylight.

"I'm not sure, but I think I have figured it out. As you see, I moved the compass to the bow, far away from the motor," he answered. Just then, his smile was quickly plucked away. He stood up. In the spare light of dawn, I could see his frozen expression as he brought the binoculars up to his face.

Martin uttered one word. "Ice," and handed the binoculars to me. A few miles away, I saw a field of solid ice stretching as far as the eye could see, to the west and to the east.

I turned away from Martin, hoping he didn't see the panic in my eyes. This was not a time to burden him with my fears. He needed my support.

Martin sat down hard on the bench. His eyebrows were knotted as he struggled with a plan.

"We don't have much time to waste. I'll set a half-hour to search the west for the boundary of the ice field. Then another thirty minutes to the east."

"Can we afford an hour or two worth of fuel?"

"We have no other choice. Hopefully we'll spot a break wide enough to channel through."

The mood on the boat became somber. One younger boy was on the brink of hysteria. Others seemed resigned that this might be the end. But Martin's orders came with assurance and his words of hope lifted us out of the gloom.

We navigated first to the west. All eyes were glued to the edge of the ice field, as if we could will it to break apart for a passageway. Nothing.

We turned back and began the trek east. All hope faded when our time ran out. Undaunted, Martin steered the boat hard up against the ice and ordered three of us with oars to the bow. His strategy was to test whether there might be any flaws in the ice that could be broken up for a channel. None was found. Only solid ice.

Then, unexpectedly up ahead, I spied movement. Yes, the ice was cracking, and slowly, very slowly drifting apart. It was the phenomenon we were seeking.

"Thank God!" Martin shouted.

We turned sharply into the narrow channel and as the boat moved, the ice moved, and magically, a channel opened up.

Bundled bodies hung over the railing everywhere, trying to protect the sides of the boat from the sharp edges of the drifting ice. We struggled with everything at hand to keep the ice from crushing into our fragile shell, kept together only with wooden plugs.

From the light breeze coming from the northeast, we knew the vastness of ice was moving, but how fast, we couldn't tell. Neither could we tell if and when the wind would change its direction.

At the moment, I was wrestling with my oar to keep the jagged ice away. I stammered, "What will happen, Martin, if the wind changes and the ice closes the channel?"

Martin straightened up and faced me. His reddened eyes met mine for only a moment before his eyes turned back out to sea. After a long pause he whispered, "We'll be crushed."

From the bilge Martin seized a long-shafted ax, and aimed, demolishing a sharp corner of the ice on the starboard side.

In an instant, my fear was gone. Gripping the heavy oar, my hands gained new strength, and at that moment I sensed the same faith and the same hope as when we left shore.

Martin moved from man to man, spreading courage as well as wisdom from his experience at sea and his knowledge of ice and weather in the Baltic.

"Look at the clouds. They're light and slow. The horizon in the west is clear, a good sign."

At the bow, I saw three of our young men encouraging a fourth to climb up and stand on their shoulders. A loud outcry reached everyone's ears, "I see ice-free waters to the north!"

"How about east and west? Do we still have channel far ahead of us?" Martin asked.

"Yes, and it seems to be wider further in our direction to the North."

"Good," Martin said, gulping in the cold air. "Let's increase our efforts. We have a chance now. I'm going to start the motor."

With a yank on the starter string, the motor sputtered and hissed, but came alive. Smiles broke out all around. That one moment almost convinced me that reaching Finland was a reality.

In half an hour, the channel was wide enough to maintain an even motoring speed. In another thirty minutes, we left our bondage behind us.

No ships. No airplanes in sight. We must still have been miles from the shipping lanes. Relaxed, we set about eating our lunch, a feast of dry fish, hardtack and water.

Martin assured us that we were on course. Our journey was now straight to the north. I volunteered to sit at the rudder and give Martin a much needed rest, while another took my place as lookout.

My eyes scanned the glittering expanse of sea with no land in sight. There was not even a suggestion of a breeze and I wondered how far our fuel would take us. Would we run into drift ice again? The enemy would have difficulty in spotting us because of the low profile of our boat.

Hours later, my lookout and I were still awake and alert. Proudly, I watched our human cargo, some napping, some in deep sleep. I glanced at Martin, who was leaning back on the railing a few feet forward from the motor. As I looked at his face, I wondered if he was really asleep, even if his eyes were closed. In spite of his youth, Martin's face expressed the ruggedness of a seaman with many years of experience. I felt secure letting him sleep for one more hour. My lookout tried to find wind and what direction.

With a start, Martin woke up, glanced at his watch and said, "We must have passed the midway point some time ago. I'm glad you didn't see any patrol boats out there."

He reached for the tiller and took command. I dropped down close to the motor and fell asleep.

Hours later, "Land!" burst from the mouths of everyone in the cramped boat. Now fully awake, I jumped to my feet.

"Land!" I repeated.

"Calm down, we're still far from the land we seek," I heard Martin say. "What you see out there are the outermost skerries, the Finnish southwest archipelago, hundreds of islands we have to navigate between and beyond before we reach our destination." He dropped his head into his hands and rested his elbows on his knees. Not a word was heard from the bunch of young men huddled close to each other in a circle near the motor well.

After awhile, I moved closer to Martin and quietly whispered, "How much gasoline do we have left?"

"I don't know," he answered. "I emptied the last can into the tank several hours ago."

"What then?" I gasped.

"We'll have to row." Martin studied the horizon with his piercing eyes. To the northwest in front of us the sky had darkened. The sea had lost its shine. In a couple of hours, at dusk, we neared the archipelago. Thankfully, the old motor still thumped away.

As darkness set in, the view of the infinite number of islands faded away and the heads of young men withered into their clothing.

Sitting close to me, Martin said in a hushed voice, "Axel, in the fore peak you'll find a lantern. Pump it up and see if you can light it."

After some struggle, the lantern ignited and shone down on the motionless men huddled in a ring at the bottom of the boat.

"Hoist it up," he signaled with his white handkerchief. Minutes earlier when sitting beside him, he had explained that he was sure we had left Hanko Peninsula behind to the east. He thought we were near the waters guarded by the Finnish coastguard. In spite of all the islands now shielding us from enemy vessels, we still had a good chance to be spotted and rescued by the Finnish coastguard.

I had barely raised the lantern when the motor stopped dead. Every head popped out of its hiding place.

"Our fuel is gone." Martin's voice penetrated the darkness. "We're drifting." He slumped over the tiller in despair.

I couldn't let fear paralyze me now. I fastened the lantern to the bow so I could help row.

Just then, I heard a very faint sound. A motor, a boat, but not visible yet, probably hidden behind an island nearby. We stopped wrestling with the oars. No one moved. Minutes passed. The sound seemed to come closer. But in front of us we saw only growing waves catching the reflective light from the quarter moon.

Then out of the shadows we spotted a vessel. Its course was dead on. The beam of its dimmed searchlight hit us. Cautiously now, the vessel inched towards us. Was the patrol boat German or Russian or Finnish?

Minutes passed, second by second.

Then I saw the flag. It was white with a blue cross. Finnish!

I looked at Martin, the one who had guided us this far. His worried brow softened as the burden of the last day fell visibly from his body.

The captain stood on the bridge. We waited breathlessly for his next move. Then with a booming voice he cried, "Throw the line!"

Relief mixed with joy overwhelmed us.

It was over.

The heavy hemp rope was not just a rescue line, but a line to freedom.

Afterword

From the Finnish Coastguard boat, we disembarked at the harbor and were taken to an old school building, where others who had escaped were housed. Waiting to be processed, the weeks dragged by, and I had time to reflect on my life and what lay ahead. I clearly remembered that day many years ago when I cried for joy in our attic on Ormsö. And again, I thanked God for allowing Mr.Linse to cross my path. Finally, I boarded a ship to Sweden.

After completing my pre-med at Uppsala University, I finished my medical studies and graduated with an M.D. degree in 1950 from Karolinska Institute, Stockholm.

Gradually, the restrictions of socialized medicine collided with my free spirit and that faraway land that I once dreamed about dominated my thoughts. I felt compelled to seek a new beginning.

After five years of practicing medicine in Sweden, I gathered my family and sailed to America, a land of opportunity for my three small boys.

It was mandatory that I take the sixteen exams necessary to obtain a medical license in the State of Washington, so I needed to learn English quickly. After my residency in surgery at Providence Hospital, Seattle, where many kind people showed me the "ropes", I obtained a position as Orthopedic Surgeon at Western State Hospital where I worked for four years.

My independent spirit nudged me again, resulting in opening a private family practice in Tacoma 1961. I was privileged to serve my wonderful patients until my retirement at the end of 1990.

In 1998, I was fortunate to visit Ormsö for the first time since my escape to Finland in 1944. It was an emotional, bittersweet journey, but it deepened my desire to complete this book.

These days you may find me behind my desk writing, or if you look carefully, you might see me in the woods of my yard, tending to hundreds of trees grown from seed obtained in my home country. My father's love of nature has truly been passed on to me.

I shall always be grateful to God that I was born on this island where I learned to live a simple life and as in Matthew 6:19, 20, to appreciate what cannot be seen nor touched.

First visit back to Ormsö in 1998, standing on the very spot from which I escaped in 1944.

ORDER PAGE

Is there someone you know who might enjoy this book?
Additional copies at $12.95 may be ordered by contacting the publisher:

>Ravenwood Publishing
>4113 35th Ave. Ct. N.W.
>Gig Harbor, WA 98335
>253-851-3565

For credit card orders, visit
www.onceuponanisland.com